D0043604

Also by Mortimer J. Adler

Dialectic
What Man Has Made of Man
How to Read a Book
A Dialectic of Morals
How to Think About War and Peace
The Revolution in Education (with Milton Mayer)
The Capitalist Manifesto (with Louis O. Kelso)
The New Capitalists (with Louis O. Kelso)
The Idea of Freedom (2 vols.)
The Conditions of Philosophy
The Difference of Man and the Difference It Makes
The Time of Our Lives
The Common Sense of Politics
The American Testament (with William Gorman)
Some Questions About Language
Philosopher at Large
Great Treasury of Western Thought (edited with Charles Van Doren)
Aristotle for Everybody
How to Think About God
Six Great Ideas
The Angels and Us
The Paideia Proposal (on Behalf of the Paideia Group)
How to Speak / How to Listen
Paideia Problems and Possibilities
  (on Behalf of the Paideia Group)
A Vision of the Future
The Paideia Program (with Members of the Paideia Group)
Ten Philosophical Mistakes
A Guidebook to Learning
We Hold These Truths
Reforming Education: The Opening of the American Mind
  (edited by Geraldine Van Doren)
Intellect: Mind Over Matter
Truth in Religion
Haves Without Have-Nots
Desires, Right & Wrong
A Second Look in the Rearview Mirror
The Great Ideas: A Lexicon of Western Thought
The Four Dimensions of Philosophy
Art, the Arts, and the Great Ideas

Adler's Philosophical Dictionary

MORTIMER J. ADLER

A TOUCHSTONE BOOK
Published by Simon & Schuster

TOUCHSTONE
Rockefeller Center
1230 Avenue of the Americas
New York, NY 10020

First Touchstone Edition 1996

TOUCHSTONE and colophon are registered trademarks
of Simon & Schuster Inc.

Designed by Irving Perkins Associates

Manufactured in the United States of America

10 9 8 7 6 5 4 3 2 1
10 9 8 7 6 5 4   (Pbk)

Library of Congress Cataloging-in-Publication Data
Adler, Mortimer Jerome.
    Adler's philosophical dictionary / Mortimer J. Adler.
        p.   cm.
    Includes bibliographical references and index.
    1. Philosophy—Dictionaries. I. Title.
    B945.A2863A3   1995
    103—dc20   95-7
                                                           C

ISBN 0-684-80360-7
      0-684-82271-7 (Pbk)

To Philip W. (Tom) Goetz,
my friend and closest associate on
Encyclopædia Britannica's
Board of Editors

Acknowledgments

Upon completion of my last book, *Art, the Arts, and the Great Ideas,* my good friend and colleague Max Weismann, cofounder and director of the Center for the Study of Great Ideas in Chicago, urged me to undertake the writing of this book. His conviction was that not only would this book represent a summation of my philosophical views, but it would afford readers, when read with my other works, an invaluable guidebook on how to think about the future.

I would also like to acknowledge my colleagues at the Institute for Philosophical Research, John Van Doren and Otto Bird, who read and criticized the entries in this book, and my assistant, Marlys Allen, who presided over the preparation of the manuscript.

Contents

Preface

In the middle of the eighteenth century, Voltaire wrote and published a work that he entitled *A Philosophical Dictionary*. He never allowed his name to be affixed to it as its author. A very much abridged translation of it by Theodore Besterman was published as a Penguin Classics edition in 1972.

In French the work runs to seven or eight volumes. Very few of the entries are philosophical. For the most part they are revolutionary diatribes, sarcastic and witty animadversions on the institutions of established church and state. But the book is in the form of a dictionary since all its entries, long and short, are arranged alphabetically.

Likewise, Diderot's *Encyclopedia* was not an encyclopedic work but a collection of articles of a revolutionary character, distinct from the *Ency-*

clopædia Britannica, a factual exposition of knowledge at the time.

I have borrowed from Voltaire nothing more than the title. This work is a dictionary in the sense that its entries are alphabetically arranged. But it is also genuinely philosophical. My purpose in writing the entries is to establish a precise meaning for the words of common, everyday speech.

In the last thirty years or so I have written thirty or more philosophical books, intended for the general public, men and women whose special vocation is not philosophy but who nevertheless regard philosophizing to be everybody's business. Unlike the works of professors of philosophy who write books and journal articles for other professors to read, these books have been written for everyone to read. In writing them, I have tried to avoid all technical jargon, all words not in the vocabulary of everyday speech.

Unfortunately, many of the words in that vocabulary are used in many senses, most of them imprecise, wrong, or inadequate. It becomes necessary to give these ordinary words the precision they should have when they are used for philosophical purposes.

The dictionary functions as a summary of the philosophical work I have done in the last thirty years, for in it I refer, wherever necessary, to the books I have written that at greater length make the points under consideration. These books are listed in Appendix I, arranged according to the subject referred to. Appendix II is an alphabetical listing of my books referred to in the dictionary.

At the beginning of Western philosophy in Greek antiquity, in the fifth book of his *Metaphysics*, Aristotle listed a large number of words that were used in a diversity of senses in that book. They were not alphabetically arranged, and Aristotle's intention was merely to explain his own usage. But the result was something like a dictionary.

ABSOLUTE AND RELATIVE The words "absolute" and "relative" are generally misused. At this time and in the present state of our culture, to affirm absolutes and assert that not everything is relative goes against the grain of popular prejudice. The popular prejudice is, for the most part, unenlightened. The difference between what is absolute and what is relative needs to be clarified.

A moment's consideration of the word "relative" should help anyone to see that what is relative is called so because it stands *in relation* to certain conditions or circumstances.

The absolute is that which *does not stand in relation* to any conditions or circumstances. It prevails at any time or place and under any circumstances. Thus, for example, the truth that atoms are divisible or fissionable is absolute, but the judgment we may make that that statement is true or false is relative to the time and place at which it is made.

For most of the past centuries the greatest physical scientists would have said that if atoms exist, they are indivisible. Relative to the time and place at which that judgment was made, and to the knowledge available at that time, the judgment had relative truth, but it is still absolutely true, at all times and places, that atoms are divisible or fissionable.

The related distinction between the objective and the subjective might be considered here. Objective is that which is the same for you and me and for every other human being. Subjective is that which differs from one person to another. The objective is absolute; the subjective is relative to individual human beings.

Finally, these two distinctions (between the absolute and the relative, and between the objective and the subjective) bring to mind a third distinction—between matters of truth and matters of taste. That which belongs in the sphere of taste rather than truth includes everything that is relative to the circumstances of different times and places. Matters of taste are those which differ from culture to culture and from one ethnic group to another, such as modes of salutation and preferences in cuisine, in dance, in customs. But if anything is absolutely true when it is entertained without any human judgment, such as the divisibility or fissionability of atoms, that truth is transcultural.

At present, mathematics, the physical sciences,

and technology are transcultural. Whether we think that history, the social sciences, and philosophy will become transcultural in the future depends on how we view them now—either as bodies of knowledge or as matters of unfounded opinion.

ABSTRACT AND CONCRETE The words "abstract" and "concrete" are used loosely in everyday speech. Concrete terms are logically those terms which refer to sensible particulars. A particular is an individual that is of a certain kind; and being of a certain kind is a member of a class. Sensible particulars are apprehended at once by sense-perception and by the intellect unless we are conceptually blind. Then these are apprehended only by the senses.

Such conceptual blindness occurs when the sensible individual thing is apprehended by one sphere of sense-perception and not by another, as when that which is perceived is not understood at all. For example, a person who is conceptually blind in his or her sense of touch may be able to identify the object by the sense of smell. This happens when a person cannot identify the kind of object it is by touching it, but can do so by smelling it. When it is just touched by this person, the individual sensible thing is a raw individual, perhaps in some way familiar, as having been touched before, but without an identity, a name.

When we are not conceptually blind, the terms "flower" or "pencil" name certain things that are both perceived and also understood as being of a certain kind. Human apprehension differs radically from the purely sensible apprehension of brute animals that do not have intellects. For them, the world consists of raw individuals. We cannot imagine how the world of sensible objects appears to them.

In human apprehension, which is both sensitive and intellectual, the abstract object of thought is one that cannot be instantiated. We call the object of thought abstract if we cannot give particular instances of it that are sensible.

Such words as "freedom" or "justice" name objects of thought that cannot be perceptually instantiated. They are, therefore, abstract in their referential significance.

In short, concrete terms are those which can be perceptually exemplified or instantiated; abstract terms are those which cannot be perceptually exemplified or instantiated. They refer to objects that are purely objects of conceptual thought.

ANALOGICAL SPEECH: ITS DISTINCTION FROM UNIVOCAL AND EQUIVOCAL SPEECH The words "analogical," "univocal," and "equivocal" are not generally used. But they are of great importance philosophically. Philosophers are concerned with the different senses in which we attribute characteristics to a number of things; or, to speak of this matter grammatically, they are concerned with the different ways in which we apply a predicate to two or more subjects.

For most people, the only distinction with which they are concerned is that between the univocal and the equivocal. They are seldom aware that they are saying anything analogically. The only thing that should be clear to us is that we all do need to be aware that we sometimes speak in a manner that is neither univocal nor equivocal, especially if we venture to speak about God and his creatures, or about material and spiritual things.

We speak univocally when in naming things we use a word with exactly the same meaning. If in a field of cows, we use the word "cow" in the plural to name this cow, that cow, and every other cow that we can see, we are using the word "cow" in exactly the same sense every time we use it. Similarly, if we call all the cows animals, we are using that word in the same sense when we use it to characterize all the cows.

Equivocation is of two sorts: equivocation by chance and equivocation by intention. Equivocation by chance occurs infrequently in the everyday use of language. It happens when the same word is used to name two things which have nothing whatsoever in common—which are alike in no respect whatsoever. That one and the same word should have such strange ambiguity can often be explained in terms of the history of the language, but sometimes no explanation can be found.

For example, the word "pen" is used equivocally by chance when it is used to name, on the one hand, an enclosure for pigs and, on the other hand, a writing instrument. Similarly the word "ball" is used equivocally by chance when it is used to name a football or a basketball, and also used to name a festivity where an assemblage of persons will be found dancing.

Equivocation by intention occurs when a person uses a word in its literal sense, on the one hand, and in a figurative sense, on the other hand. When the Russian Emperor was called the father of his people, the word "father" was being used in a figurative sense. The Emperor stood in relation to the Russian people in a manner that bore some comparison to the relationships between a father, who is a biological progenitor, and his progeny or offspring.

Words used in a metaphorical sense are usually words that are used equivocally by intention. Every metaphor is a condensed simile. To call the Russian Emperor the father of the Russian people is to say that he stands in relation to them *like* a biological progenitor to his progeny.

I have already said that we speak analogically in a manner that is neither univocal nor equivocal—using a word in neither the same sense, nor in different senses, when the senses are related (as in equivocation by intention) or unrelated (as in equivocation by chance). Yet at first glance what I am calling analogical speech looks somewhat like equivocation by chance. It is certainly not univocal speech.

The example that Aristotle gives for speech that is analogical involves the same word applied to objects of the different senses. Take the word "sharp." We speak of a sharp point when the sharpness is in the sphere of touch. We speak of a sharp sound when the sharpness is in the auditory field; and of a sharp light when it is in the visual field.

In these three cases, we are using the word "sharp" in a manner that appears to be equivocal; but it is not, because the different senses of "sharp" when we use the word in these three ways derive from the differences between the subjects of which we predicate "sharp." In addition—and this is the distinguishing mark of the analogical—we find it impossible to say what it is that is common to these three uses of the predicate "sharp." We cannot specify what the sharpness is that makes it proper to speak of a sharp point, a sharp sound, and a sharp light.

The importance of this point should be clear to persons who speak of God and human beings and other of God's creatures. We recognize that we are not using the word "exists" in the same sense when we say that we and other things exist and that God exists; but we cannot specify the difference between God's mode of being and our mode of being except negatively. We know it is not the same.

We know that in the sense in which God exists, we do not exist; and in the sense in which we exist, God does not exist. The word "exists" is used analogically of God and God's creatures. Similarly, the word "knows" is used analogically when we say that we know and that God knows. The difference between the two meanings of a word used analogically is like the difference between two words being used equivocally, but here the equivocation is not by intention nor is it by chance. It is derived from the difference between the two subjects to which the word is applied.

Turning from theology to philosophy, we use the word "generalization" analogically, if we speak of the kind of generalization that occurs in the sphere of animal or perceptual intelligence and in the sphere of human or conceptual intelligence. If brute animals do not have intellects and human beings do, then if we ever use the word "concept" for what is in the minds of animals and what is in the human mind, when both animals and human beings solve problems by

21

thinking, we are using the words "concept" and "thinking" neither univocally nor equivocally, but analogically.

ANALYTIC AND SYNTHETIC JUDGMENTS

Modern philosophy is suffering from the mistake that Immanuel Kant made in his distinction between analytic and synthetic judgments. According to Kant, an analytical judgment is a verbal tautology. It is uninstructive. We learn nothing from it, for the predicate is contained in the meaning of the subject. To assert that lead does not conduct electricity merely asserts that it is true that lead is classified as nonconductive metal.

In contrast to all such verbal tautologies or noninstructive propositions are judgments of the mind that are based on empirical evidence. Here, according to our experience, we affirm a proposition in which the predicate is independent of its subject. An example of a synthetic judgment is that hot bodies cool off by radiating their heat to the environment.

To assert that all judgments are either analytic

or synthetic is to deny that there are any judgments that are neither analytic nor synthetic in Kant's sense of the term. These are judgments in which both the subject and the predicate are indefinable terms, such as "whole" and "part." You cannot say what a whole is without mentioning parts; nor can you say what a part is without mentioning wholes. The foregoing statement introduces us to the meaning of self-evident propositions.

A self-evident proposition is one in which the opposite is unthinkable. We cannot think that the whole is less than any one of its parts or that a part is greater than the whole to which it belongs. The proposition that the whole is greater than any of its parts is certainly instructive as well as being self-evidently true.

There are not many propositions that are self-evidently true. Among self-evident truths, the most important is the law of contradiction: nothing can be and not-be at the same time. Nothing can have an attribute and not have it at one and the same time.

The philosophical and scientific thought of Western civilization is governed by this rule of noncontradiction, a rule that instructs us that we ought never to affirm two propositions that cannot both be true. If truth is the agreement of the mind with reality—with the way things are—then the logical rule prohibiting contradiction reflects the self-evident, ontological principle that contradictions do not exist in reality.

Mystics, Western as well as Eastern, may embrace contradictions and even think that the ultimate nature of reality is replete with contradictions. The Zen Buddhist Master teaches his disciples how to give contradictory answers to the questions he asks. But if the Zen Master is flying from Tokyo to Kyoto he will be willing to fly only in a plane whose aeronautical engineering is based on physical science that is governed by the principle of noncontradiction.

ANARCHY What most people have in mind when they use the word "anarchist" is the image of a bomb-throwing revolutionist. They do not know about the existence of philosophical anarchists.

The philosophical anarchist is one who mistakenly believes that human beings can live together peacefully and harmoniously without government. He denies the necessity and indispensability of government for the existence of society.

The following example will show why this is an error. Let us suppose three scientists are going off to explore the jungles of the Amazon River. Before they depart, they must agree on some principles that they unanimously accept as governing their decisions while they remain together. Either they must appoint one of them as their leader and agree to abide by his or her decisions, or they must agree on majority rule and abide by the decisions of any two of them against the third. Unless they unanimously accept one or the other of these two principles governing their making of decisions, they will not get very far before they become disunited and at odds. The mission that they are undertaking will fail.

Marxist thought includes the vision of a time when the state and coercive government will wither away and society will endure thereafter peacefully without the existence of coercive government. The dictatorship of the proletariat was thought to be only the penultimate stage in the communist revolution. The ultimate stage was envisioned as an anarchist society—one from which the evils of government and coercive force had been totally eliminated.

Anarchy exists in the world today only with respect to sovereign states. A sovereign prince or state is one that admits no governing superior. Two or more sovereigns in their relation to one another do not constitute a harmonious or peaceful society. In fact, sovereigns are always in a state of war, even when they are not engaged in actual warfare. As Thomas Hobbes correctly observes, war consists not only in actual battle, but in a tendency thereto among sovereigns. We have come to call that state of war, which does not involve actual warfare, as a "cold war." (*See* the entry under War and Peace.)

The League of Nations after the end of World War I in this century, and the United Nations after World War II, were steps in the direction of peace, but they did not go far enough. Only if a world federal government were eventually established in the future, a government that would possess a monopoly of coercive force, would we have a state of global peace from which the anarchy of sovereign states and their state of war with one another would be abolished.

ANGELS Most people who use the word "angels" have before their minds the image they derive from paintings of winged creatures robed in white. This is far from the proper meaning of the word "angel" to denote an immaterial substance—a spiritual being.

In taking this view, Thomas Hobbes employs a eulogistic and dyslogistic criterion of meaningful speech. He says, in effect, that when anyone speaks of immaterial substances, such as angels, they are making no sense whatsoever. A name denoting that which does not and cannot exist is nonsense.

There is no philosophical proof of the existence of angels. It is an article of religious faith for Jews, Muslims, and Christians. But the denial that angels exist and the further statement that they are impossible is sheer dogmatism on the part of materialists.

What the materialists do not understand is that we cannot prove a negative assertion, such as *angels do not exist*. What is affirmed without proof is dogmatically asserted if it is not self-evident that angels are impossible and cannot exist. It is not self-evident that the immaterial is impossible; hence the dogmatism of materialists remains.

The discussion of angels properly belongs to theology as an exposition of the articles of religious faith. The philosophical interest in angels is mainly concerned with what I have called "angelistic fallacies." Blaise Pascal tells us that man is neither angel nor brute. It is unfortunate that he who would act the angel, acts the brute.

Those who, like Plato and Descartes, are dualists affirming that there are both material and immaterial substances—body and soul, for Plato; *res extensa* and *res cogitans* for Descartes—cannot avoid committing angelistic fallacies by attributing to the human intellect properties it does not have. Thinking that the human intellect is an immaterial substance, they cannot avoid thinking of it as if it had angelic properties.

There are four angelistic fallacies. The first is angelistic politics. Alexander Hamilton tells us that "if men were angels, no government would be necessary." What he should have said is that if men were angels, coercive force would not be necessary to sustain the rule of law.

There are other reasons for government that apply to angels as well as to men. It is the philosophical anarchist who commits this angelistic fallacy, thinking that some principles of government—either the rule of a leader or majority rule—are not indispensable for making decisions. Even a peaceful society of angels or men involves deciding matters that are morally neutral—neither intrinsically right or wrong—and so require some rule to decide. (*See* the entry under Anarchy.)

The second fallacy is in psychology. It is telepathy. Angels, if they exist, communicate with one another through nothing physical, such as human speech. Angels communicate with one another telepathically. There are parapsychologists who claim that one man can read the mind of another by telepathy; that is, without the intervention of spoken or written words. Telekinesis is another phenomenon that some parapsychologists describe. It consists in moving a physical thing without touching it, not using any physical means to do so.

The third fallacy is angelistic linguistics. The German philosopher Gottfried Leibniz committed this fallacy when he conceived the possibility of inventing a language, which he called a "Universal Characteristic," from which all ambiguities are removed. By using this language, human beings would be able to communicate with one another as angels do, without any chance of misunderstanding.

The fourth fallacy is angelistic ethics. Plato asserts that knowledge is virtue—that if one knows what one ought to do, one will also do it. This assertion may hold true of angels who do not suffer from an intrinsic conflict between their lower and higher faculties, between their sensitive appetites and their reason, but it is not true of human beings, who have such faculties.

Not being angels, human beings can be incontinent in Aristotle's sense of that term. They often allow their passions to prevail over their reason, and so they often confess their remorse about having done what they know they ought not to have done, or failing to do what they ought to do. Such remorse does not afflict angels.

Aristotle is not a dualist as Plato and Descartes are, but he does assert that the human intellect is distinct from all the sensitive faculties. It is an immaterial power. This assertion poses for Aristotelians the problem of where humanity stands with regard to the boundary that separates the material world from the spiritual—the realm in which God and angels exist.

An easy solution to this problem would place man in both realms—in the physical by reason of his body and the senses; in the spiritual realm by reason of his intellect. But that is not quite correct. Man stands at the dividing line with both his feet and the rest of his body planted in the material or physical realm. Standing thus, he manages to lean over that line looking into the spiritual realm by the powers of his immaterial intellect.

ART In everyday speech and on everyone's tongues, the two words that are generally misused are "art" and "love," and of these two, the word "art" is probably misused more.

I call attention to the variety of misuses of the word "art" and of the related phrase "the fine arts." People seem to be unaware of the contradictions into which they fall when they allow themselves to say the things they do.

In the first place, the word is used for paintings that hang on the walls of museums called "museums of art," or statues that stand on pedestals there. These things are not art, but they certainly are works of art. They are also frequently referred to as works of fine art. But the museums of art contain many things that are not paintings or sculptures, such as suits of armor, swords and javelins, and Greek vases.

31

In the second place, college catalogs usually include phrases such as "literature, music, and the fine arts." Is not a poem or novel a work of art? Is not a musical score a work of art? And, furthermore, are not poetry and music as well as works of visual art, all works of fine art, whereas the pottery, the swords and armor, are works of useful art?

In the third place, whom do we call artists? Only persons who produce works of visual art or anyone who produces anything or who performs in any manner with acquired skill? Do we not call all great pianists and opera singers artists?

Human beings are artists, and almost everyone is an artist in making something or in doing something. Cooks are artists; so too are seamstresses and plumbers, grammarians, equestrians, navigators, generals of armies, fly fishers, and drivers of automobiles.

In this fundamental use of the word "art" for the skills that human beings have in producing something or performing in a certain way, we do not distinguish between the various arts as liberal, useful, and fine. A moment's thought about the etymology of the English word "art" would have prevented anyone from misusing the word for what human beings produce instead of for their skill in producing it.

The English word comes to us from the Latin *ars,* and that word is a translation of the Greek word *technē,* which is best rendered in English by the word "skill" or by the phrase "know-how." Thus understood, art is one of the intellectual virtues, a practical intellectual virtue as contrasted with theoretical intellectual virtues, such as understanding, science, and wisdom.

One thing further needs to be clarified, and that is the phrase "fine art" wrongly identified with the works of visual art that are found in museums. At once we can see that the word "fine" is not being used as an adjective. The categorization of some works as works of fine art does not exclude other works as *not* excellent and so *not* fine at all.

Here we are helped by the phrases in German or French that are used to categorize the works of art that in English are called works of fine art. In German the phrase is *schöne Kunst;* in French, it is *beaux arts.* Where, then, does the phrase "fine art" come from?

My guess is that it comes from the derivation of the word "fine" from the word "final." Works of fine art are final in the sense that they are not to be used as means to ends beyond themselves, but rather to be enjoyed as ends in themselves. The useful is always a means; the enjoyable is an

33

end. The fine arts are the arts productive of the enjoyable. When a Sheraton chair is put on a platform and behind ropes it is viewed as an enjoyable work of fine art, in addition to having originally been made as a useful means for sitting down.

AUTONOMY The Greek etymology of the word "autonomy" tells us that it is being a law unto itself—not being governed by any superior on earth.

It is worth commenting here on a mistake we find in Rousseau's *Social Contract*. In a hypothetical state of nature, and so in the absence of society, every human being has the freedom of autonomy. But when they enter freely into the social contract, Rousseau says they are still as autonomous as before.

No one in a political society is autonomous. The citizens who obey the laws in the making of which they have a voice enjoy political freedom, but political freedom is not the freedom of autonomy—the freedom of people in a state of nature; rather it is to be governed with one's own consent and with a voice in one's own government.

What Rousseau calls "a state of nature" is not natural if the word "natural" is used in Rousseau's sense that refers to a hypothetical state of nature. Instead, it is both natural and conventional. It is natural by need; human beings need political society in order to live well; and at the same time it is conventional, not by a social contract, but rather as constituted by such men as Solon and Lycurgus, who respectively gave constitutions to Athens and to Sparta.

When this meaning is understood, certain passages in Aristotle's *Politics,* Book I, Chapter 2, which at first appear to be contradictory, become intelligible without contradiction. In other words, human beings cannot achieve a good or *civilized* life unless they are citizens of a state, but the states that are thus constituted differ conventionally from place to place.

BEATITUDE In Christian theology, the word "beatitude" means the eternal happiness of the blessed who achieve salvation and are in the presence of God. It is of importance philosophically by virtue of the difference between eternal and temporal happiness. In this life and in time, happiness is not attainable, for it is a normative rather than a terminal end. (*See* the entry under Happiness.) But those who see God are immovably in a state of heavenly rest. (*See* the entry under Heaven and Hell.)

It is impossible to imagine heaven or heavenly rest or give concrete meaning to the phrase "see God." However, we find ourselves using the word "rest" in a sense beyond and different from sleeping or not being actively engaged in some venture. The Book of Genesis says that God created the world in six days and on the seventh day He rested. We also know that the Sabbath is a day of rest. What does this statement mean? Certainly not that God is inactive on the seventh day, or that we should do nothing on the Sabbath.

I suggest it means contemplation and worship. On the seventh day God contemplated his creation and found it good. On the Sabbath, our being at rest involves us in prayer and worship. We are at rest when we rise above everything practical and temporal. Resting on the Sabbath is a foretaste of heavenly rest or beatitude.

Still one other temporal and secular way of understanding rest is the aesthetic experience. When we behold that which we find beautiful, we have an experience that in time is analogically like the beatitude of seeing God.

BEAUTY In everyday speech, when people use the noun "beauty" or the adjective "beautiful," they use it to mean something they think is fine or wonderful—almost a synonym for the word "swell." They do not think of the sense that these words have in philosophical aesthetics.

St. Thomas Aquinas' definition of beauty as that which pleases upon being seen tends to support subjectivism. For "being seen" read instead "being beheld," and then what Aquinas is saying is that which, when beheld, gives us pleasure, we call beautiful. Different persons get pleasure of this sort from different objects. They differ in their tastes. What one person finds enjoyable, another might behold with no pleasure at all.

However, there is another aspect of beauty that most persons fail to consider. In addition to the enjoyable, there is the admirable. What makes one object more admirable than another is some excellence in the object itself. That which is more admirable may not also be more enjoyable.

This brings us to the interesting question of whether human beings differ from one another in the matter of taste. Can we say that some persons have good taste or that some persons have better taste than others who have poor taste or no taste at all?

Is it not true that the only way you can know whether a person has good taste or poor taste is by the fact that individuals who have the best taste are those who enjoy the most admirable objects? Is this not the only way you can judge a person's degree of taste? If you can rank objects in the degree to which they are admirable, then the individuals who find the more admirable also the more enjoyable will be persons of superior taste.

If there are those who still doubt that there is an objective aspect of beauty as well as a subjective aspect, or who question the concurrence of the enjoyable and the admirable, let them be asked whether it is possible to spoil a work of art that many individuals find enjoyably beautiful.

If they admit that the work of art can be spoiled—that is, made less admirable—then they are acknowledging that there are certain traits of the objects in question that can be altered or removed to make it less excellent, that is, less admirable. The traits in question are in the object, not in the senses of the beholder.

That is what it means to say that admirable beauty is objectively present, but enjoyable beauty is in the eye of the beholder, who gets pleasure from beholding it.

The three things that everyone should remember when they think about beauty are (1) the distinction between enjoyable and admirable beauty; (2) the scale that places individuals according to the degree to which they have good taste, enjoying most that which is most admirable; and (3) admirable works of art can be spoiled by removing from them those traits which, when present, make them objectively excellent and admirable.

BEING The word "being" is an understanding of that which in the twentieth century is identified with reality.

What does the word "real" mean? The sphere

of the real is defined as the sphere of existence that is totally independent of the human mind. The familiar distinction between appearance and reality calls our attention to the fact that there is sometimes a difference between the way things appear to us and the way they really are—the character they have apart from our cognition of them.

Immanuel Kant was correct in thinking that the history of philosophy would be divided into two periods—before and after Kant. In the two thousand or more years before Kant's Copernican revolution in philosophy, no one questioned the existence of an independent reality and, except for a few extreme skeptics, no one doubted that reality was both knowable and intelligible. Beginning with Kant, such realism ceases to be prevalent, and for the first time what might be called "ontological idealism" takes its place. Before Kant, no other philosopher was an idealist. Idealism is a peculiarly modern error, one that is widely prevalent today and one for which we are indebted to Kant.

This is not the place to explain how Kant made this mistake, except to say that it would not have occurred to him did he not think that Newton's physics and Euclid's geometry expounded the truth with certitude, and so they needed to be defended against Hume's mistreatment of them. Suffice it to say, now that Einstein has supplanted Newton and now that we have non-Euclidean geometries, Kant's attempt to give Euclid and Newton certitude is an ingeniously contrived theory of how the innate structure of the human mind imposes on our experience the form of space that is Euclidean and the kind of causality that explains Newton's celestial mechanics. But it is nothing more than an ingenious contrivance, and it can be dismissed as no longer necessary or sustainable.

Kant does not deny the existence of reality. The thing in itself—the *Ding an sich*—exists, but it is unknowable. Being independent of the human mind, it lies outside all possible experience, which is given its shape and all its features by the human mind.

In the period before Kant, the treatment of being took its main terms from Aristotle's *Metaphysics* and from the *De Ente et Essentia (Of Being and Essence)* of Thomas Aquinas. Today, when the leading philosophers are idealists rather than realists, we are mainly concerned with the way things appear to be as opposed to the way they really are.

We are, therefore, called upon to face a problem that Sir Arthur Eddington states for us in the opening chapter of his Gifford Lectures on *The Nature of the Physical World.* The table in front of him, he says, is solid and impenetrable to his hands that lean upon it. But he tells us that, from the physicist's point of view, it is nothing but a field of empty space, a void in which elementary particles are moving about with great speed.

How can the same table be both what it appears to be to our ordinary sense-perception and what it really is according to the physicist's theory of it? I shall summarize my solution of the problem. The elementary particles exist really only when they exist in a cyclotron, not when they are organized as the constituents of all the physical things that are the objects of sense-perception. In the latter case, the elementary particles are only *virtually* present, and that virtual existence can be turned into actual existence only by destroying the physical thing in which they are virtually present.

Ever since Kant, philosophers have vainly tried to prove the real existence of the external world—the world outside our minds. A correct understanding of perception shows why such efforts are vain as well as unnecessary. Except for the mental act of perception, all other acts of the mind, such as imagination, memory, and conception, present us with objects concerning which we must ask whether, in addition to being objects of the mind, they also exist in reality. But in the one case of perception, we cannot separate our having the perceptual object before our minds from asserting that it also really exists.

If that were not so, there would be no distinction between hallucinating and perceiving. Hallucination is pathological. Normal perception is always the perception of something that has existence in reality. If we do not assert that the perceptual object also really exists as a perceptible thing, we cannot say that we are perceiving it. No proof of an external world is necessary.

Existence has three modalities. The first is real existence, existence independent of the human mind and unaffected by it. The second modality is subjective existence. The contents of the human mind, its sensations, perceptions, images, memories, and concepts, have existence in your mind and mine. Since you and I really exist, subjective existence is also one form of real existence.

There is a third modality—a third mode of existence that is neither totally independent of the human mind nor totally dependent on the individual mind. This third mode is the existence of all the objects of the human mind except perceptual objects. Other than perceptual objects, we must always ask whether they have real existence as well as objective existence, that is, existence as intended objects, the objects that the human mind intends or means.

This third mode of existence is a middle ground between real existence and subjective existence. Real existence is existence independent of mind; it is the existence that physical things had before there were human beings on earth. Intentional existence is not independent of the human mind, but it is also not dependent on the existence of any one individual mind, as subjective existence is.

Objects that exist for two or more minds, objects that they can discuss with each other, have intentional existence. If there were no minds on earth, there would be no objects that had intentional existence. To summarize this middle ground between real existence and mental existence, it consists in (1) not being dependent on the acts of any particular human mind, and in this respect it differs from subjective existence, and (2) not being independent of the human mind in general, and in this respect it differs from real existence. It is a mode of existence that depends on there being some individual minds at work.

Another distinction with which we must deal is that between being and becoming, between the mutable being of all things subject to change, and the immutable being of that which is timeless and unchangeable. That is eternal which is beyond time and change. In the realm of change and time, past events exist only as objects remembered, and future events exist only as objects imagined.

Here we must take account of necessary and contingent beings; and among contingent beings, some are subject to transformation, as a human being is when an individual dies and turns into dust and ashes. A contingent being may be radically contingent; only the cosmos as a whole is radically contingent. The cosmos can be otherwise in character; and it is self-evidently true that that which is capable of being otherwise is also capable of not being at all—of being replaced by the null and void, by nothingness.

Finally, we must consider the distinctions between the possible and the impossible. The latter is that which is incapable of being. In the sphere of the possible, we must further distinguish between *entia reale* and *entia rationis*. The latter are fictions of the mind, such things as mermaids, centaurs, and unicorns, and also such fictional characters as Antigone and Hamlet.

We should be shocked by Stephen Hawking's bold as well as erroneous statement that what is not measurable by the physicist has no existence in reality. In the same book in which Professor Hawking makes that statement, he also frequently refers to the mind of God, which is certainly not measurable by the physicist. Either he is referring to something that has no reality, or he is wrong in saying that those aspects of time which are not measurable by the physicist have no reality. (*See* the entry under Time.)

BELIEF In any religious community that has an articulated creed, the first words uttered when the creed is recited are "I believe." The various things thereupon recited are the articles of religious faith. That is the primary meaning of the word "belief." It stands for things affirmed that lie beyond all philosophical knowledge or opinion, as well as beyond science and history.

The demonstration of God's existence, if it is

valid philosophical knowledge, is said to be a preamble to faith rather than an article of faith. In the three great religions of the West—Judaism, Christianity, and Islam—the first article of faith is that sacred scripture is the revealed word of God.

There are, of course, beliefs that are not religious faith. William James tells us about things he cannot affirm as knowledge but which he does affirm by exercising his will to believe. Unable to resolve the issue about the freedom of the will, a matter that troubled him greatly, he derived great comfort from willfully believing that human beings had freedom of choice.

To affirm this freedom, in his view, was beyond all evidence and reason. Others similarly settle for belief in God, or in the immortality of the soul, by exercising what James called the will to believe. Such affirmations tend to be stronger and firmer convictions than the knowledge we have or the opinions we hold by empirical evidence and rational argument.

The element that is common to religious faith and nonreligious belief is its voluntary aspect. Both involve an exercise of the will. Being willing to believe is what distinguishes both religious and nonreligious faith from knowledge and right opinion. The will moves the reason to affirm

47

what reason cannot establish by its own power. (*See* the entries under Knowledge and under Opinion.)

When religious faith is thought of as a divine gift, the will is moved by God to affirm what lies beyond the natural powers of the mind to acknowledge. The will is supernaturally moved. For those who have a faith that is not religious, the factors that move the will are natural, not supernatural.

CAPITALISM AND SOCIALISM The words "capitalism" and "socialism" are of recent origin in everyday speech—as recent as the nineteenth and twentieth centuries. The words are generally misused by most individuals. One flagrant misuse occurs when no distinction is made between socialism and communism. Then the latter is used to designate state capitalism as contrasted with private-property capitalism.

The Soviet Union and the countries controlled by it (what was then East Germany, Poland, Czechoslovakia, Romania, and Hungary) were all capitalist countries in the descriptive sense.

That is, they were all *capital-intensive economies* in the same way that the Western constitutional democracies are.

The difference between these two kinds of capital economies was that in the Eastern bloc, state capitalism prevailed. As prescribed by the Marxist–Leninist doctrine, the private ownership of capital was abolished. All capital, agricultural as well as industrial, was owned by the state and was administered by the Communist Party. The political result was a totalitarian state—no private economy and no private institutions. The economic aspect of the Western democracies involved the private ownership of capital and a market economy.

Let us consider constitutional democracy as an ideal that the various countries in the West, as well as India and Japan in the Far East, approximate in different degrees. The ideal approximated can be stated as a society in which all adult human beings are political *haves*; all who have reached the age of consent are citizens with suffrage and have political liberty. They are governed with their own consent and have a voice in their own government. Citizens in public office have more political responsibilities to discharge and so have more power than ordinary citizens, but all are equal as citizens.

49

The economic counterpart of this political ideal is socialism. Socialism is an ideal, as democracy is, and it is approximated in varying degrees. As an ideal it is the economic face of political democracy. The ideal is approximated in a society in which all mature citizens are economic as well as political *haves*. It is a society with no economic have-nots—no one deprived of a decent livelihood, to which every human being has a natural right.

In the same way that all citizens are political *haves,* they are all economic *haves.* That is why democracy and socialism are two faces of the same coin. Among the economic *haves,* some will have more and some less in terms of the contribution they make to the economy. But all are equal at the baseline in which all have enough to live a decent human life.

The mistake made by Marx and Lenin was thinking that abolishing the private ownership of capital was an indispensable step in the direction of the socialist ideal. On the contrary, private ownership of capital and a market economy are indispensable means to the socialist ideal. They are required for the production of enough wealth to distribute so that everyone's right to a decent livelihood can be realized.

Though Marx and Lenin had the socialist ideal in mind, they took the wrong steps to realize it. They ended up with a totalitarian state and a failing, nonprosperous economy.

CASUISTRY As the word itself suggests, we are here concerned with particular cases. When the moral law or the principles of ethics are applied, they are applied to particular cases, each one unique in the circumstances and factors that are operative in the here and now.

Aristotle in Book V of his *Ethics*, on justice, points out that general rules do not apply perfectly to particular cases; and so an equitable dispensation from the general rule is required to do justice in the particular case.

In the tradition of the Anglo-American common law, the separation of courts of law from courts of equity, which were the province of the Chancellor, provided an institution that enabled justice to be done in the particular case, justice that departed from the general rule.

One way of saying what is sheer dogmatism in

the ethics of Immanuel Kant is to point out that his moral law—his so-called categorical imperative—completely ignores the circumstances of particular cases. According to Kant, there are no exceptions whatsoever to the general rule that lying violates one's moral duty to tell the truth.

We are to imagine the following case. A man is standing at his fence on the roadside. He sees an individual breathless and haggard with fear running down the road, as if pursued. A little beyond his house, the road on which this individual is running branches into two forks, one to the left and one to the right. The individual running away pauses for a moment and then decides to take the fork to the left.

A moment later, two villainous-looking individuals brandishing big clubs appear and ask the man who is still standing at his fence whether the man they are pursuing with deadly intent came by and, if so, which fork in the road beyond the house he took.

Should the onlooker tell them the truth though he can be almost certain that if the pursuers catch the man who is fleeing, they will do him in with their clubs and fists?

Without knowing whether the individual who is fleeing from his pursuers is guilty or innocent of some crime, and without knowing anything about the motivation of the pursuers, Kant answers the question of whether the onlooker should tell the truth flatly in the affirmative. Kant does not allow for any casuistry whatsoever. No moral philosophy that does not provide casuistry for finding exceptions to general rules can be sound.

There are many other reasons for finding fault with the moral philosophy of Immanuel Kant, but the dismissal of casuistry is sufficient in itself to challenge the validity of Kantian ethics.

CAUSE *See* the entry under Certainty and Probability.

CERTAINTY AND PROBABILITY The words "certainty" and "probability" do not apply to propositions that are either true or false. These propositions entertained by us with suspended judgment should never be qualified as either certain or probable.

In the Anglo-American common law there are degrees of certainty and doubt. Certainty attaches to judgments beyond the shadow of doubt; not certain are judgments made with a reasonable doubt; and less certain still are judgments made by a preponderance of the evidence.

The last two are judgments to which some degree of probability must be attached, the former more probable, the latter less probable.

The propositions in each of these two cases, when entertained with suspended judgment, are either true or false. Certainty and probability qualify our judgments about the matters under consideration, not the propositions entertained with suspended judgment.

This statement brings us to consider what happens by chance and what is causally determined. Here we must distinguish between the mathematical theory of probability and the philosophical theory of what happens by chance. In the mathematical theory of probability, which begins with an essay by Blaise Pascal, one can calculate the chances of anything happening by the number of possibilities present; for example, in the toss of a coin, the chance of its being heads or tails on any toss is fifty–fifty, because in the long run, with many tosses, that is how one should wager on the next toss, if we know that the coin being tossed is not affected by any extraneous factors.

In the philosophical theory of probability, what happens by chance is what happens without a cause. Consider the coincidence of two individuals who happen to meet on a particular street at a particular time. Why do we call this a coincidental meeting, and regard it as an uncaused event?

The answer is that each of the two individuals is caused to be at that spot where the chance meeting occurs by all the causal factors operating in his own past, but nothing in their separate pasts causes them to meet each other there. The coincidence is, therefore, an uncaused or a chance event.

While we are dealing with caused and chance events, let us spend a moment on the Aristotelian theory of the four causes—the material and the formal cause, the efficient and the final cause.

In all works of human art, the four causes operate—the material cause is the nature of the materials on which the artist operates, the formal cause is the productive idea in the artist's mind, the final cause is the end or purpose that motivates the artist to produce the work of art, and the efficient cause is the action of the artist's hands and tools. But when we depart from the sphere of artistic production, final causes do not operate. What happens naturally happens without any purpose or end to be served.

The critics of Aristotle in modern times who denied teleology or purpose in the physical world were correct in dismissing final causes, but they were incorrect in dismissing the operation of material, formal, and efficient causes in the works of nature, corresponding to those in works of art.

In human activity, free choice as well as physical causes operate. Freedom of choice is present when, in deciding on any activity, the individual could have chosen otherwise. His action is, therefore, causally determined by the exercise of his willpower rather than by the kind of causes that operate in nature.

Human freedom of choice does not make the chosen decision an uncaused decision, but the operative efficient cause is not like the efficient causes that operate in natural phenomena, which are determinative but unwilled.

It is, therefore, incorrect to think that there is an irresoluble conflict between free will and causal determinism. The freely chosen decision is causally determined, but not in the same way that events in the physical world are causally de-termined.

CHANCE *See* the entry under Certainty and Probability.

CHANGE The word "change" is a synonym for the word "becoming" and an antonym for the word "being." In the entry under Being, I discuss the antithesis between the mutable and the im-mutable, the realm of the changeable and the realm of the unchanging or permanent. Not everything that is unchanging is eternal or time-less, as God is.

Things that come into being and pass away have a permanent being while they are subject to all forms of accidental change, such as change of place, change of quality, and change in quantity. For example, the apple that reddens on the sunlit tree is, from moment to moment, the same apple, otherwise it could not be said to be an identical object undergoing change in color or size.

This leads to the distinction between substantial and accidental change. The birth and death of animal organisms is substantial change; their motions from place to place, their changes in quality and quantity, are accidental changes.

That which changes substantially in coming to be and passing away does not change from being to nonbeing. Substantial change is rather an alteration in mode of being, a kind of transformation, as when a living organism becomes a decaying corpse. In the physical cosmos nothing passes away absolutely; nothing violates the laws of conservation.

When it is said that God creates *ex nihilo,* nothing or absolute nonbeing is the antecedent of the created cosmos. But when animal organisms procreate offspring, they are generated from preexistent seeds. (On this point, *see* the entry under Being.)

The importance of this point is that if the cosmos were ever to cease to be, the consequence of this change would be nothingness or absolute nonbeing. That radical change is not a transformation of being, as the decaying corpse is. It is being's negation or denial.

CHOICE *See* the entry under Certainty and Probability.

CITIZEN The word "citizen" is inseparable from the word "constitution." Only when a government is constitutional, only in a republic, are there some individuals who are citizens. It may be that only some of the people are governed with their consent and with political liberty; or it may be that, except for certain justifiable disfranchisements, all human beings constitute the people who are governed with their consent, and who have political liberty.

First there are those who are governed as slaves, governed without their consent, without participation in government, and for the good of their masters, not for their own good.

Second, there are subjects: individuals who are governed despotically because they are thought incapable of participating in government. Those who are infants or below the age of consent are governed despotically, but the despotism is benevolent if the parents are concerned with the welfare of the progeny they rule. Adults of a conquered people are despotically governed as subjects, sometimes benevolently, sometimes tyrannically, for the good of the ruler rather than for the good of the subjects.

In various epochs and places before the liberation of women, female adults in oligarchies with restricted suffrage were governed despotically as subjects. The first step toward their emancipation was granting them suffrage. They then became citizens.

Universal suffrage makes citizens of all who are above the age of consent and participate in their own government. That gives us the definition of citizenship. It belongs to those who are given political liberty and equality, those who are governed with their own consent and have a voice in their own government. All citizens are politically free. They are not all politically equal, however, for in constitutional governments citizens may be temporarily or permanently in public office. When that is the case, they have more political power than those who are not in public office, because they have more political functions to discharge.

Another way of defining citizenship is to speak

of citizens as having a share in sovereignty. As citizens, all have an equal share.

The existence of citizenship depends upon the existence of constitutional government, but that government need not be democratic, as the government of Athens was not democratic in the fifth century B.C., and the government of the United States was not democratic in the eighteenth and nineteenth centuries. Both were oligarchies with unjustly restricted suffrage. The populations included slaves and subjects as well as citizens; those who were citizens consisted of a minority of the population. Democracy comes into existence only with universal suffrage, which gives citizenship to all who by natural right are entitled to it. (*See* the entries under Constitution and under Democracy.)

CIVIL DISOBEDIENCE What are the conditions that justify dissent from civil government, and how does justifiable disobedience to civil government differ from rebellion?

One ground for civil disobedience is religious. Quakers who regard killing in war as sinful disobey the draft laws by being conscientious objectors. At the same time, they do not withdraw their consent to civil government, and they voluntarily submit to the treatment that their government inflicts on those who refuse to be drafted.

Another ground for civil disobedience may be that the deserter regards the war being fought as unjust. The conscientious objector in this case refuses to participate in it. Again, the individual must be willing to take whatever treatment is accorded those who disobey the law.

Disobedience to civil government may also involve withdrawal of consent. When it is peaceful, that act requires emigration, as with those who opposed the war in Vietnam, and went to Canada or Sweden for the duration. They required a declaration of amnesty to return to the United States and resume their status as citizens.

Violent disobedience constitutes rebellion or civil war. This resistance is civil in name only, since the authority of the government is not only denied but resisted by resort to arms.

Our war of independence and our civil war were acts of rebellion, involving denial or rejection of civil status by those who opposed the government. Nevertheless, Lincoln's declaration of amnesty to the rebellious population of the southern states restored them to citizenship in the republic, in effect nullifying their rebellion.

CLASSES, KINDS In the twentieth century we use two words for that which in the Middle Ages were called *universals*. Instead of saying that every common name in the vocabulary of English or other European languages signifies a universal, we say that it signifies a class or kind. This naming holds not only for nouns but also for adjectives and the participles of verbs.

The obvious question is, how do such universals—classes or kinds—exist? Individuals, particular things, or events we perceive, imagine, or remember exist in the physical world. They are signified by all the proper nouns we use or when, in the place of a proper noun such as "George Washington," we substitute a definite description, such as "the first President of the United States."

The answer to the question posed is, first, negative. Classes or kinds do not have real existence, the kind of existence that you and I have. They do not have mental existence—the existence in our minds of cognitive mental content (which in modern times we misuse the word "ideas" to designate).

Positively, then, we must say that they have objective or intentional existence. (*See* the entry under Being.) They exist as objects *of* the mind, not as items *in* the mind. They exist for any two human beings who have before their minds an object that they can discuss.

In modern times, in the writings of Bishop George Berkeley and David Hume, the objective or intentional existence of kinds or classes is denied; and also denied is the mental existence of what Berkeley and Hume called "abstract ideas." For them, only words have general significance, applicable to two or more individuals that have some characteristic or trait in common. This error on their part is called "nominalism." (*See* the entry under Nominalism.)

COERCION AND DURESS Free choice is voluntary action, the very opposite of the compulsory. What is called coercion occurs when individuals are compelled by force to do something that they would not do voluntarily.

The individual who surrenders his wallet to a thug who holds a revolver to his head does so under compulsion and involuntarily. He is being coerced. Police who enforce the law against criminals exercise coercive force.

If all individuals obeyed the law voluntarily because they acknowledged its authority and its justice, there would be no need for coercive force. Because they do not, coercive force must be used to enforce law in a population that includes individuals who do not acknowledge its authority and justice.

What about those acts which no one would do voluntarily, but which, nevertheless, are not done to avoid the threat of coercive force. Are they done voluntarily or involuntarily?

In his *Nicomachean Ethics,* Book III, Chapter 1, Aristotle considers the action of the captain of a ship who throws his cargo overboard in order to save his ship in a storm at sea. Is he acting voluntarily or involuntarily? Clearly, it is not involuntarily. The captain is not compelled to jettison his cargo under the circumstances, but under those circumstances, he thinks it preferable to jettison the cargo rather than lose his ship.

The word "duress" is used for such actions

that partake of both the voluntary and the involuntary. Another word that might be used for such actions is "nonvoluntary." It applies to actions that partake of both the voluntary and the involuntary. The captain could have chosen otherwise under the circumstances. His choice, being free, is voluntary.

All of us who act under duress, act voluntarily and by free choice. We are not compelled or coerced, but we also do something that no one would regard as desirable.

COGNITION The word "cognition" refers to the contents of the mind *by which* we know or understand the world about us. But the contents of the mind are not all cognitive.

Examples of noncognitive mental contents are our bodily feelings, our pains and aches, as well as our emotions and sentiments. We are directly aware of such noncognitive mental content. A toothache is not *id quo,* but *id quod*—something that we directly apprehend rather than that by which we hold some object before our minds.

This definition raises a question about whether

we can converse with others about our pains and aches. The dentist I talk to about my toothache has no experience of it. It is mine alone. I can describe it to him and he can understand my words, but he cannot feel it.

If communication involves having a shared object to discuss, then is my conversation with my dentist about my toothache communicative? Strictly speaking, the answer is *no*. But if my dentist ever had a toothache himself, he can imagine what a toothache is like while I am talking about the toothache I am now having. To that extent, we can be communicating even if the toothache is not the same object for both of us.

COMMON GOOD Most people use the phrase "common good" as if it were a synonym for the general welfare. There are two common goods, but in different senses of that word. In Latin they are called *bonum commune hominis* and *bonum commune communitatis*.

The first of these is identical in meaning with happiness. It is common in the sense that it is the same in essence among all human beings. (*See* the entry under Happiness.) When I say it is the same in essence for all human beings, it may differ from individual to individual only in accidental respects and in degree.

The other, the *bonum commune communitatis*, or the good of the social community, is a means, not an end. It is common in the sense that all individuals, in their pursuit of happiness, must employ it as a means to that end.

This means to happiness is common in the sense that all human beings share in it. They should all aim at it, each individually according to the individual differences that differentiate them.

For example, the peace of the society is an aspect of the common good of the community. Everyone should act to procure a peaceful community. Another aspect of the community's good is justice in the treatment of society's members. Each individual should work to procure justice for all; so, too, liberty for all and the equality of all.

COMMUNISM AND SOCIALISM To the entry
under Capitalism and Socialism I add here some
comments on the seventy-year experiment with
communism in the Soviet Union.

Though Lenin and Leon Trotsky, apostles of
Karl Marx and Friedrich Engels, aimed at the socialist ideal in 1917, the communist experiment
defeated their attempt to produce a truly democratic and socialist society. Until Mikhail Gor-
bachev and Boris Yeltsin appeared on the scene
in the 1980s, the Communist Party did not realize
that neither democracy nor socialism could be
accomplished by abolishing the private ownership of capital and by preventing a free-market
economy.

Lenin had said, of course, that the dictatorship of the proletariat under the despotic regime
of the Party was the penultimate stage of the
revolution. It was necessary while the Soviet
Union was surrounded by their capitalist ene-
mies. The ultimate stage of the revolution lay in
the future, when the state had withered away.
Lenin's *The State and Revolution* is very clear on
this point, but wrong in its predictions. Many
individuals in the United States think that com-

munism and socialism are identical. In fact, they are antithetical.

CONSTITUTION In everyday speech, most Americans use the word "constitution" as if it referred to the Constitution of the United States adopted at the end of the eighteenth century, ratified and amended since then. It is connected in their minds with the word "citizen." There are no citizens except in republics, whether only some human beings have the suffrage or all are enfranchised.

What, then, is a constitution, either oligarchical and unjust or democratic and just?

Aristotle's *Politics,* Book I, Chapter 2, tells us that a constitution is an arrangement of political offices, designating the powers of the various offices and their responsibilities. A constitution determines who shall be admitted to citizenship, how the other offices shall be filled, and how the different offices should function in relation to one another.

The constitution may be a written document.

If so, the act by which the people adopt the constitution is an act prior to the existence of government. That fact raises an interesting question about Lincoln's dating of the birth of the United States in 1776 rather than 1791, when George Washington took office as the first President of the United States.

Another interesting question is whether there is constitutional government in the United Kingdom. The laws made and changed by Parliament give the government of the United Kingdom the appearance of constitutionality, but unless a government is constituted before it begins to function, the word "constitution" is ambiguously applied to governments with written and with legislatively enacted constitutions. The former are prior to the institution of government; the latter are *posterior* to the existence of government.

The most important feature of constitutional governments lies in the distinction between a government of men and a government of laws. When a human being governs by power which he is able to exercise and which is vested in him or her personally, we have a despotic government, whether tyrannical or benevolent. But when those who govern not by their personal power, but by the power vested in the office they hold, assigned to that office by the constitution they swear to uphold, then the government is a government of laws. Constitutional governments can, in time, change, becoming less oligarchical and more democratic. The mode of amending constitutions must be prescribed by the constitution itself.

Officeholders are not the governors in constitutional government, but rather the people who adopt and amend the constitution. It is they who, as citizens under the constitution, vote and elect those who administer the government.

The government resides in the power of the people who have been made citizens. The officeholders in Washington and elsewhere are its administrators. They are the servants of the people. We acknowledge that fact when, after national elections that change the party in office, we talk about a new administration, not a new government.

CONTEMPLATION In Book X of his *Ethics*, Aristotle compares the life of action with the contemplative life, and declares the life of the philosopher to be higher because it is contemplative.

This declaration, it seems to me, is a Platonic error on Aristotle's part. For Aristotle the final end is happiness, the *totum bonum* or complete good—all the things that are really good for human beings. The *telos* or final end must be the same for all members of the species. The *bonum commune hominis* must be achievable in different degrees by all human beings. It cannot be an end that ought to be pursued by some, but not by all.

If the final end is the same for all human beings, what is the highest of the goods that comprise it? In the *totum bonum,* what is the *summum bonum*—the highest good among all the real goods that comprise the *totum bonum*?

The answer cannot be contemplation in the first place because only God is the proper object of contemplation; and in the second place because being able to contemplate God is itself a gift of divine grace.

In this life and apart from religion, the secular form of contemplation occurs when human beings contemplate things of beauty, either in nature or in works of art. The contemplation of the beautiful is, by analogy, the secular counterpart of religious contemplation on earth and of the beatific vision in heaven.

What, then, is the highest good, in which all human beings can participate in varying degrees? It is intellectual work, discursive thought, work that is self-rewarding. The intellect is man's highest power, and good use of it is the highest good.

The good use of the intellect is learning, and all the activities by which we learn and grow intellectually are acts of pure leisuring—not toil, not subsistence work of any kind unless it is admixed with leisure, not play or amusement, but work that is genuinely creative. A life that does not involve leisuring is not a good life. It is leisuring, not contemplation, that is the highest good.

CONTINENCE AND INCONTINENCE

We cannot understand what it means to say that man is a rational animal without, at the same time, recognizing that a rational animal is a freak of nature. The nature of a rational animal is a mixture of incompatible elements.

The animal aspect of human nature motivates us to seek sensual pleasures. The rational aspect controls our conduct by counseling us to desire nothing amiss. In consequence, man is the only living organism in whose *nature* conflict exists, conflict between the animal and rational aspects of our nature.

Evidence of such a conflict we cannot deny. That we all experience remorse indicates that we often do what we later recognize to be wrong. We also often fail to do what we later recognize we should have done.

Individuals who act as reason dictates and in doing so control their sensual appetites are continent. Truly virtuous persons who have cultivated habits of right desire do not for the most part need to be continent, but even they may be faced with a conflict in their desires that call upon them to be continent rather than incontinent.

Were this not so, individuals would never experience remorse for having done what they ought not to have done or for having failed to do what they ought to have done. (*See* the entry under Casuistry.) Only saints, persons of heroic virtue, are the exceptions, but it is likewise they who know and can say that there, but for the grace of God, go I.

CUSTOM AND CONVENTION As the word "convention" indicates, what is conventional is in the realm of the voluntary. The institutions that human beings voluntarily institute are the products of nurture, not nature.

That which is natural is the same everywhere, but positive laws and customs are conventional. As the Greek sophists said, fire burns here and in Persia, but the laws and customs of the Persians and of the Greeks are different.

On many aspects of human conduct the laws enacted and enforced by those who have the authority or power to do so are silent. Where the laws are silent in a community, customs that have existed from time immemorial have the force of law. In the development of the English common law, for example, what is established by ancient customs prevails.

DEMOCRACY The word "democracy" is misused both in academic and popular speech to name any form of government in which the many rather than the few have a voice in government. As thus used it is distinguished from oligarchy, and it is possible to say that democracy began in ancient Athens under the regime of Pericles. Philosophically speaking, the word "democracy" applies to a form of government that first appeared in the twentieth century.

In the United States, that appearance is as late as 1964, when the Twenty-fourth Amendment to the U.S. Constitution was adopted, abolishing the poll tax and creating truly universal suffrage.

But still belonging to the future is the economic basis of democracy—that other face of a truly democratic society which secures the right to a decent livelihood to which all citizens are entitled. This is the proper meaning of socialism.

Only when all mature and normal citizens are economic *haves* as well as political *haves*, with some *haves* having more and some having less according to their contribution to the economy, will we have a working approximation to the ideal of a socialist democracy.

This news will shock the many who think that the democratic ideal first made its appearance in ancient Greece. In his funeral oration, Pericles praises Athens for instituting democracy at a time when, in an Athenian population of 120,000, only 30,000 were citizens and the rest were disfranchised women, artisans, and slaves.

In our twentieth-century understanding of political democracy, Athens was a constitutional oligarchy, not a democracy. Individuals make the same mistake when they think that in the eighteenth and nineteenth centuries, the Constitution of the United States was democratic rather than oligarchic.

Lincoln insisted that a new nation "conceived in liberty and dedicated to the proposition that all men are created equal" came into existence in 1776 with the Declaration of Independence, not with the Constitution of 1789, which allowed slavery. But he recognized that the Declaration expressed a hope for a future that in fact began to be fulfilled only in the twentieth century. (*See* the entry under Constitution.)

There are four main forms of government: tyrannical despotism, benevolent despotism, constitutional oligarchy, and constitutional democracy. According to the principles of justice, it can be argued that only the last of these is the best form of government, because only it embodies all the principles of political justice.

Tyrannical despotism is totally unjust, because

the de facto rulers govern with no one's consent, with no one's participation, and for their own good rather than for the good of the governed.

Benevolent despotism acknowledges that the good of the governed should prevail. The welfare and well-being of those subjected to benevolent despots is the end that government should serve. Nevertheless, that benevolence is curtailed by a despotism that denies the right of human beings to be governed with their consent, with a voice in their own government, and with all their natural rights secured.

Constitutional oligarchies, varying from place to place and from time to time in the numbers of persons who are enfranchised as citizens, are more just than any despotism, tyrannical or benevolent, because at least some human beings have political liberty and the equality of citizenship. Such governments remain unjust to the extent that the rest of the population are governed as subjects or as slaves.

When finally in the twentieth century truly universal suffrage was established, we saw at last a form of government that is demonstrably democratic and completely just. If any injustice remains for the future to abolish, it is the economic justice of the socialist ideal.

DOGMATISM   Most people use the word "dogmatism" in its dyslogistic sense. They forget that
the word "dogma" has a good meaning in dogmatic theology, referring to the articles of religious faith.

In philosophy, however, dogmatism is totally
inappropriate. Everything that is asserted or denied must be submitted to rational inquiry that
seeks to establish it with certitude or probability.

There are some philosophical positions the affirmation of which are beyond the power of reason to establish. An example is the main thesis of
ontological materialism, that nothing really exists except bodies and their physical transforma-
tions. That thesis, being a denial, therefore is a
negation, and as such it is indemonstrable.

Most of the contemporary scientists and professors of philosophy who embrace materialism
unquestioningly do so without a logical qualm.
They mistakenly think that the evidence of their
senses tells them that all observable phenomena
are physical. Of course this is correct, but it does
not prove that only observable phenomena are
real. There is no evidence that reality does not
and cannot include the immaterial and the
nonphysical. To assert that it does not and can-

not is sheer dogmatism, of a kind that should be avoided in philosophy.

DUTY The word "duty" is used in philosophy as a synonym for moral obligation. As so used it requires us to understand wrong and right uses of the phrase "categorical imperatives." Immanuel Kant's use of that phrase is an instance of extreme rationalism in moral philosophy. (*See* the entry under Casuistry.) A truly categorical imperative is one that is self-evident. It is derived from the understanding of prescriptive truth.

All the main propositions of moral philosophy are prescriptive rather then descriptive. They are statements of what ought or ought not to be sought and done. In short, they are statements of our moral obligations or duties.

The one categorical imperative is that we ought to seek everything that is really good for us, and nothing else. Seeking goods that are merely apparent goods is permissible, but not obligatory.

The categorical imperative, or first principle of moral philosophy, is self-evident. It is impossible to think that we ought not to seek what is really good for us, or that we ought to seek what is really bad for us. The words "really good" and "really bad" coimplicate the words "ought" and "ought not."

If a moral philosophy is formulated entirely in terms of ends and means, it is utilitarian or pragmatic. It is an ethics without duties or moral obligations. The word "deontological" is philosophical jargon for an ethics or moral philosophy the principles of which are imperatives that prescribe duties.

A moral philosophy can be both pragmatic and deontological. Aristotle's *Ethics* is both. Ends and means are certainly present in it, but it also contains principles that are prescriptive of duties or moral obligations.

The moral philosophy of Immanuel Kant is wholly deontological. It rejects what Kant calls "the serpentine windings of utilitarianism." J. S. Mill's *Utilitarianism* contains the opposite error: it is purely pragmatic, and has great difficulty with the notion of duty or moral obligation.

EDUCATION The word is used so loosely that to talk about "education" without qualifying adjectives attached to it is not informative; or worse, it is misleading.

The qualifying adjectives I suggest are "general" and "special," "preparatory" and "continuing," "terminal" and "unending." Most people think of education as something that goes on in educational institutions, schools, colleges, and universities. They regard persons who have earned a diploma, a certificate, or a degree as individuals who, to some extent, have been educated.

They forget that individuals learn a great deal with little or no schooling. They forget that experience teaches, and that learning by any means is part of a lifelong educational process. Schools of all grades and kinds are only one group of means in the pursuit of education.

A much better question to ask is: Who is a generally educated human being? The negative answer is easy; certainly not any person who has just earned a diploma, a degree, or some other sort of certification.

Youth itself is the greatest obstacle to becoming a generally educated human being. Schooling at its best is preparatory. In addition, it is often specialized, preparing individuals for some form of skilled work or for professional expertise. Finally, it is terminal: it can be completed in a relatively few years.

When the school is liberal, when it trains individuals in the liberal arts that are the arts of learning, it is preparatory. Those who are liberally trained to read and write, speak and listen, measure and calculate, have acquired the skills to go on learning after they have graduated; but unless they continue to learn year after year, they are likely never to become generally educated human beings. If the liberal training they receive in school includes a taste of all the major disciplines, they will have some awareness of what there is to learn in order to become generally educated by the end of their lives.

Becoming a generally educated person is a lifelong process. It is an unending pursuit of learning, concluded by death but never finished or terminated by death. In my judgment, sixty is the age at which one can begin to become generally educated, on condition, of course, that the process has been continuing after all schooling has been finished.

After age sixty, one is fully mature and experienced, has been challenged by all the intricate problems of living, has done a great deal of conversing, and is finally ready to make and defend solutions to life's major problems, or to acknowledge the existence of problems to which one can find no satisfactory solutions.

Individuals whose schooling was specialized rather than liberal and who do not continue learning when they leave schooling behind, or do so only to improve their specialized expertise, never become generally educated human beings. This statement holds for most physicians, lawyers, and engineers, as well as for most professors in our colleges and universities for whom getting a Ph.D. merely indicated the field of specialization they would cultivate thereafter.

EMOTION In the tradition of Western thought the word "emotion" is generally misused for feelings and sentiments—in general, for affects. These are, in neurological and physiological terms, not emotions at all.

Aristotle's *Rhetoric* has a long list of irascible

and concupiscible emotions in pairs, each with its opposite, such as love and hate or joy and sorrow. A similar listing and grouping is adopted by Thomas Aquinas in his *Summa Theologica*. Other lists are presented by Benedict Spinoza in his *Ethics,* Book IV, where they are called the passions and are treated in relation to human bondage and freedom. We can also find listings of the emotions or passions in Francis Bacon, Thomas Hobbes, and John Locke, and in subsequent writings by British empirical psychologists, David Hume, George Berkeley, and J. S. Mill.

A very short list of the emotions is presented in the psychology of William James, where he pays tribute to Professor C. Lange, a Danish physiologist, for his contribution to a theory of emotions that came to be known as the James—Lange theory.

According to this theory, emotions are widespread bodily and visceral changes that are controlled by the sympathetic nervous system. This widespread neurological and physiological commotion includes such things as pupillary dilation, changes in the respiratory system and in the psychogalvanic system (electricity in the epidermis), presence of adrenaline in the blood stream, and changes in the pulse. This complex state of changes, occurring simultaneously and accompanied by bodily movements of attack and withdrawal, constitutes an emotion, strictly speaking.

With two exceptions, all emotions are alike in their visceral components, differing only in the bodily actions of attack and withdrawal. Anger or rage is one of them, and fright or fear is another. They are alike viscerally but they are differentiated in the acts of attack and withdrawal that accompany the same visceral commotion.

Two exceptions are grief, on the one hand, and sexual orgasm on the other hand. These two have no opposites. There is no emotion of joy or one of love. Most of the so-called emotions (listed and grouped by the philosophers from Aristotle, Aquinas, Spinoza, and the British empirical psychologists, until we get to the psychology of William James and to the James–Lange theory of the emotions) are mild feelings, sentiments, or affects that involve no physiological, neurological, or visceral components.

I have little hope that people generally will give up making long lists of the emotions that fill the pages of literature. These lists belong to poetry, not to scientific physiology and neurology. The best word to use for the psychological states they refer to is the word "sentiment."

Sentiments represent the nonrational aspect of human nature, the aspect of human nature that human beings share with other animals. (*See* the entry under Continence and Incontinence.) The human conflict between reason and the passions that is discussed there afflicts human beings because they are like other animals, on the one hand, and unlike them, on the other. The James–Lange theory of emotions applies to the lower animals as well as to human beings, as anyone knows who has observed a hissing and ferocious cat or a frightened rabbit.

ENDS AND MEANS In most contexts, the meaning of the words "ends and means" is clear. But when these two words are used in moral philosophy, further clarification is needed.

On the side of means, we must distinguish means that are merely means and means that may be both means and ends—means to a proximate end and, in turn, means to an end that is itself a means to some further end.

We must also distinguish between constitutive

means and operative means. When the final end is the *totum bonum*—the complete whole of goods, all real goods—each of the real goods involved is a constituent or component of the *totum bonum*. The factors that function as means to leading a morally good life (moral virtue and good fortune) are operative means. They are not parts of happiness, but productive of it.

On the side of ends, we must recognize that the final end or ultimate good is that which leaves nothing more to be desired. It is not one good among many, but is itself the completely satisfying good. It is also a normative, not a terminal end.

A terminal end is one that can be reached and rested in. If one is planning a trip to Vienna, that city is a terminal end. When all the means to getting there are employed and Vienna is reached, the means–end sequence stops. But a morally good human life is a whole that cannot be realized in any time sequence; nevertheless, it can be held in mind as a goal to be aimed at.

In all the performing arts, the good to be aimed at is normative, not terminal. The conductor of a symphony orchestra has in mind a certain rendition of the symphony's four movements as he rehearses the music, but the symphony as a whole does not exist and cannot be heard at any moment in time. It can be said that it was well played only after it is finished.

The same is true of living. It cannot be said of an individual that he or she has succeeded to some degree in leading a good life until a whole life has been lived. At any period during living, the only comment that can be made is that the individual is on his or her way to leading a good life. If what happens in the time remaining is like what has happened in the time so far elapsed, it can be said in a funeral oration that he or she succeeded in having led a good life. Otherwise, changes of fortune and even collapses of virtue can occur at any time and render the life disastrous or demeaned.

If the character of normative ends is understood in this way, it will also be understood that at every moment the means chosen are the end in the process of becoming. (*See* the entry under Happiness.)

EQUALITY AND INEQUALITY The usual understanding of these words is that, in relation to two things being compared, equality exists when one is *neither* more *nor* less in some specified respect. They are unequal if, in a given respect, one is more and the other less.

The most important point to remember is that things cannot be compared in general, but only in a precisely defined respect. Thus, for example, when we say that all human beings are equal, we must specify the only respect in which that is true; namely, in their humanity.

Two things can be compared in another way. One may have a characteristic or attribute that the other totally lacks. If, for example, one is a human being possessing an intellectual power that the other, a brute animal, totally lacks, they can be said to be unequal. But when we say that human beings are equal because they all have some intellectual power, their inequality in the degree of intellectual power possessed does not negate their equality in kind.

The two distinct modes of equality and inequality are, first, equality and inequality in degree with respect to a certain attribute or trait; and second, equality and inequality in kind.

ETERNITY This word has two meanings that should never be forgotten. Most individuals use the word in common speech to refer to time without beginning or end—everlasting or endless time. In this meaning of the word, God cannot be said to be eternal, for God is not in time and so is not subject to change or mutability that characterizes all things in time.

The second meaning of eternal is to have being outside of time. Eternal being is beyond our capacity to imagine or conceive in terms that are positive. Our only sense of the eternal in this meaning of the term is negative—the negation of time. Even if we think we can imagine God, we cannot imagine His eternity.

The eternal is like the immaterial in that it can be grasped by us only in negative terms—*what it is not*. Most individuals use the word "spiritual" as a synonym for "immaterial" but they forget that the only meaning they can attach to that word is negative, not positive. The spiritual is simply that which is not material. So, too, the eternal is simply that which is not in time. The eternal is the *immutable*.

EVOLUTION Since Darwin, the word "evolution" is used in place of the word "development" for any sequence of changes in which the past contains the seeds of what occurs later. This is not confined to biological phenomena, but applies to other fields in which such sequences can be found. In these sequences there is continuity, and the direction of the developmental (or evolutionary) change is from lower to higher, from less to more complex.

Darwin himself seldom used the word. His concern was with genera and species, with genetics and heredity, with breeding and the obstacles to it.

We might be tempted to call Aristotle an evolutionist in the light of his statement that "nature proceeds little by little from things lifeless to animal life" and that "throughout the animal scale there is graduated differentiation in amount of vitality and capacity for motion."

At first blush, the theory of evolution with regard to plants, animals, and man appears to come into conflict with the first chapter of the Book of Genesis in the Old Testament. But Augustine's interpretation of Genesis 1 declares that God created all things at once in their causes, and that the temporal sequence in which different forms of life appeared on earth is the work of propagation, not of creation.

On this view we are confronted with a difficult question about *Homo sapiens*—the human species. Is man covered by Augustine's thesis that in the beginning God created everything in their causes, or is there a gap or discontinuity between man and the rest of nature that calls for acts of special creation for each individual human being? (*See* the entry under Man.)

FAITH, HOPE, AND CHARITY According to Christian theology, these three words name the theological virtues that are divine gifts to those upon whom God bestows his grace. Faith consists of beliefs voluntarily espoused, beliefs that are totally beyond the reach of evidence and rational processes. "I believe," said an early Christian, Tertullian, "because it is absurd"—that is, nonrational.

Hope is the nonrational expectation of salvation and the beatific vision in Heaven. Charity is one of the three major forms of love—the love of God and of thy neighbor as thyself.

What appears to be faith, but is not living faith because it is not accompanied by hope and charity, is a counterfeit of faith. It is the voluntarily exercised will to believe, a merely human faith, not the supernatural faith that is a gift of God. (*See* the entry under Belief.)

FRATERNITY (FRIENDSHIP) The word "fraternity" or "friendship" names one of the three major forms of love. All the forms of love involve benevolent impulses toward another; none is an expression of purely selfish desire.

Friendship or fraternity is natural, not supernatural, love, as is charity or the love of God. It is also a form of love that involves no erotic or sexual component. It is the love that a human being wills to another. The person loved is also a person in whose company one wishes to live and upon whom to confer benefits in any way possible.

If all men were friends, Aristotle tells us, there would be no need for justice. The precepts of friendly love are all positive, and the precepts of justice are mainly negative, prohibiting injury to others.

———————————————

GOD   Almost everyone uses the word "God," but almost nobody can say what they mean by the word, especially if they are pagans or persons without religious beliefs. If they are members of the three religious communities of the West—Judaism, Christianity, and Islam—they have been taught how the word is used in the dogmatic or sacred theology of their religion.

However, let us suppose that they are pagans—persons who have no religious beliefs of any kind, and let us suppose that this entry is being written by a pagan for pagans.

As an exercise in philosophical theology, how shall we give meaning to the word "God"? For one thing, we know at once that the word "God" is a proper noun and that, as with any other proper noun, we must try to substitute a definite description for it.

As with the proper noun "George Washington," we cannot be introduced to the individual named and so we cannot learn how to use it by acquaintance. Instead we must substitute a definite description, such as "the first President of the United States." (*See* the entry under Classes, Kinds.)

Another preliminary point is that we can have no empirical concept of God. We have no experience of God, as we do have of cats, dogs, whales, and horses, from which we can abstract a concept of those kinds. Of inexperienceable entities, we must form theoretical constructs. It is of the theoretical construct "God" that we must now form a definite description.

We are helped in doing this by St. Anselm. He asked himself: When I use the word "God," how do I give that word meaning? His answer was: Must I not say to myself that when I think about God, I am thinking of that than which I can think of nothing greater?

In short, the first step is to describe God as *the* supreme being. Not *a* supreme being, because there cannot be two supreme beings. Must I not also think of God as existing in reality as well as existing as an object before my mind? Hence, God must be described as a really existing supreme being.

Now any being that exists in reality either is one that came into being and passed away, or is one that necessarily exists—one that cannot *not* exist. If I am thinking of God as the supreme being, I must choose the latter—a being that cannot *not* exist.

To go further than this choice in my definite description of God, I must ask what the necessary, real existence of God is like. Three answers are possible: (1) totally unlike the existence of anything else we know as existing; (2) essentially like the existence of all the other things we know to exist; and (3) both like and unlike the existence of everything else the existence of which we know.

These three alternatives are exhaustive, and if the first two must be rejected, we are left with the third. The first must be rejected, because then the word "existence" can have no meaning for us; and the second alternative must be rejected because then God's existence would be physical, mutable, material, sensible, and we would be unable to answer the question: Why do we not know God's existence in the same way that we know the existence of everything else?

To say we know that God's real existence is both like and unlike the existence of everything else the existence of which we know is to say that when we apply the word "exists" to the things of the physical world and to God, we are using the word "exists" analogically. (*See* the entry under Analogical Speech.)

This usage requires us to say that, in formulating a definite description of God, we must first use negative words, such as "immaterial," "immutable," "imperceptible," "inconceivable," and "unimaginable." "Infinite" is another negative word we must use, and give that word meaning by saying that God is not a particular individual, not a member of any class.

But to say that God really exists and that we human beings also exist is to say something positive about God. Since anything said of God and creatures is said analogically, not univocally or equivocally, we must always add that we do not exist as God exists, nor does God exist as we exist.

Three more negative words enter into the definite description of God. They are "independent," "unconditioned," and "uncaused." God has real existence from himself alone. His very being is to exist. Whereas the existence of all dependent, caused, and conditioned physical things is *ab alio* (from another), God's existence is *a se* (from himself). The unusual word "aseity" applies to God alone.

Finally, we can ask about God's being alive, knowing, and willing. If these three positive attributes cannot be added to the definite description of God, then God is not the supreme being, for there could be a greater being than one who is not living, knowing, and willing. But when we say that God lives, knows, and wills, we must add at once what the analogical use of these words requires: the God does not live as we live, does not know as we know, and does not will as we will.

The definite description we have formulated to give meaning to the proper noun "God" does not answer the question of whether God does really exist. Anselm thought it did constitute an affirmation of God's existence—that the definite description of God made God's existence self-evident. That is an error made by Anselm and others who think that the so-called ontological argument makes it unnecessary to question whether the object that the definite description puts before our minds is also one that does exist in reality.

GOOD AND EVIL The basic pairs of words in moral philosophy are "good and evil" and "right and wrong." I am going to deal here with only the first of these pairs. (For the other pair, *see* the entry under Rights, Natural and Civil.)

The word "good" is used in a number of senses. The first is its use as an adjective, with a comparative and a superlative, as in good, better, best. This is its grading sense, in which things are judged for their exchange value. It is of little interest to the moral philosopher except in its use with regard to the *summum bonum* or the highest good, the best among all the real goods that are objects of desire. (*See* the entry under Ends and Means.)

Another sense of the word is its use as a noun, when it refers to all the goods that are objects of desire, the real and apparent goods, the goods needed and wanted.

Finally, there is a sense that is unfamiliar to most individuals. This is the ontological good— the intrinsic perfection that everything which exists possesses. Here, as Augustine tells us, a mouse has a perfection or goodness that is greater than that possessed by an inanimate stone like a pearl. Living organisms have more intrinsic perfection than inanimate and inert things, even though the latter may have greater value in the marketplace.

In this ontological sense of goodness, only God, that which no greater can be thought of, has perfection as the supreme being. Only God is perfectly good, and only complete nonbeing is absolutely evil. For everything to exist at all is to have some ontological goodness. Whatever exists has some grade of perfection in the hierarchy of beings.

In the angelic hierarchy, the seraphim Lucifer has the greatest perfection among all God's creatures; and it is that which tempts Lucifer to commit the sin of pride in wishing to know God as God knows himself. With the fall of Lucifer and the other angels that follow him, Lucifer becomes Satan, morally, not ontologically, the most evil of all creatures.

This is a clear example of the separation of moral evil from ontological perfection. A morally sinful human being still has, in terms of ontological goodness, the highest grade of perfection among living organisms on earth.

GOVERNMENT Two points are of philosophical interest here. One is the necessity of government exercising coercive force. (On this subject, *see* the entry under Anarchy.) The other point is the classification of the four major forms of government. (On this subject, *see* the entry under Democracy.)

Of these forms, the most thoroughly unjust is tyrannical despotism. The most thoroughly just is socialist democracy. Between these two are benevolent despotism and constitutional government, the latter of which is oligarchical rather than democratic.

HAPPINESS Words that are generally misused in everyday speech are like most of the words that the philosopher cannot avoid using because they name great ideas or aspects of them. In some cases another word might be introduced to remedy the ambiguity. The word "happiness" is a prime example.

There is, on the one hand, the purely psychological meaning of "happiness" when that word is used to refer to the satisfaction or contentment an individual feels in getting what is wanted. In this meaning, one can feel happy one day and not happy the next day, but in either meaning, the individual is reporting an experienced subjective feeling. The primary point to remember here is that, in their psychological meanings, happiness and unhappiness are experienceable feelings. That is not the case when we come to the ethical or moral meaning of the word.

In its ethical or moral meaning, the word "happiness" refers to a life well lived, a whole life that is morally good because it is the product of virtue (or the habit of right desire) accompanied by the blessings of good fortune.

In this sense of the word, happiness is not something we feel or experience. In no moment or period of time can happiness in this sense be felt or experienced. During one's life, one may be on the road to happiness, one may be described as *becoming* happy, but one cannot be said to be happy. Only when your life is over can someone else commenting on your life declare that you *had* lived a good life and can be described as a person who *had* achieved happiness.

Happiness in heaven and out of time is experienced in eternity and *is* experienced by those who enjoy the beatific vision. (In regard to this meaning, *see* the entry under Beatitude.)

HEAVEN AND HELL These two words are used by everyone who is acquainted with Christian religious beliefs and with Christian theology. They are also used by persons of Jewish faith and of Islamic beliefs, but not in quite the same sense.

The word "heaven" is also a term in Ptolemaic and Copernican astronomy. In that context it has changed its meaning considerably since antiquity and the Middle Ages. Before telescopes "heaven" referred to the visible sky at night; and even after rudimentary telescopes, the heavens were the visible planets of the solar system and the fixed stars.

I mention these things because in the Middle Ages, when the theological doctrine of heaven was developed, people thought of heaven in terms of the sky above them. No one then knew that our sun and the solar system constitute a very small speck in one of more than a billion galaxies.

Writing as a philosopher, I may be heretical in what I have to say about heaven and hell. If the souls of the damned and the saved are immaterial beings, then neither heaven nor hell can be a place, up there or down below. The orthodox belief is that there are two sorts of pain—the pain of sense and the pain of loss. Both sorts of pain are supposedly suffered in hell by the damned. But that cannot be true. There cannot be any sensible pain experienced by an immaterial being, though such a being can suffer the pain of loss, the loss or deprivation that is the absence of God.

In the light of twentieth-century cosmology, the word "heaven" cannot refer to a place anywhere. To go to heaven is not to go "up there." The resurrected Christ does not ascend to heaven, nor does he descend from there. And there can be no "right hand" of God, the father in Heaven.

Fundamentalists in all three of the Western religions make the great mistake of reading the words of holy scripture literally and never going beyond that. It is they who disseminate the heretical beliefs that I have criticized, not I.

From a philosophical point of view, heaven is the presence of God, where the souls of the blessed enjoy the beatific vision. Correspondingly, hell—either on earth or hereafter—is the absence of God, a great loss or deprivation.

This view of heaven and hell does not have any imagery. Dante could not have written *The Divine Comedy,* filled with pictures of hell, purgatory, and heaven, if he understood this distinction.

However, this colorless and imageless rendition of the words "heaven" and "hell" fits perfectly into St. Augustine's interpretation of the opening sentence of Genesis: "In the beginning, God created heaven and earth." According to Augustine, "heaven" stands for the whole spiritual creation—the angels; and "earth" stands for the whole physical or material creation, not just this small planet in the solar system. All place terms, all space locations, all spatial directions have meaning only in the physical cosmos, not in the spiritual realm of heaven, a realm in which there is no where or when.

HIERARCHY Those who use this word correctly use it as it applies to the hierarchy of positions in the Roman Catholic Church, and also as it applies to the hierarchy of angels.

As thus used, the word refers to a very special kind of ordered series. There are series such as the series of fractions. The series of fractions is said to be continuous.

In contrast, a hierarchical series is not continuous. The series of integers is discontinuous in the sense that there is no number between one and two, between two and three, between three and four, and so on.

The only status among the prelates that is both higher than a priest and lower than a bishop is that of monsignor. In other words, the hierarchical order of positions in the Roman Catholic Church is like the order of the integers, with a small finite number, in which the status of the Pope is highest, with which this hierarchical series ends.

In the case of the angels, which are minds without bodies, the hierarchy, topmost of which is Lucifer, the highest seraphim, includes nine orders of angels—seraphim, cherubim, thrones, principalities, powers, and so on, down to the lowest order of angels, which are the guardian angels, an order just beneath the archangels. In each of the nine orders, the angels belonging to that order are arranged hierarchically. To understand this order, one must remember that each angel is a species, not an individual belonging to a species, as you and I are individual members of the human species.

When the word "species" is used philosophically by Aristotle to name the substantial forms that inhere in a number of individuals, he tells us that the order of the species, or substantial forms, is like the order of the integers.

The word "species" is also used for the members of botanical or zoological taxonomy. In the biological sciences, the word is used in this sense, and there are hundreds of thousands of species of plants and animals.

But in the philosophical sense of the word "species," there are at most five species of substance—elementary inanimate substances, composite physical substances, and three species of animate substances—vegetative, sensitive, and rational.

The human species is the highest because it is rational. Aristotle tells us that this is a discontinuous series like the series of the integers, not like the series of fractions between zero and one.

HISTORY Everything in this mutable world of changing things has a history. Its history consists of its factual development in reality.

But there is another sense of the word "history" when it is used as the name for a kind of literature. Thus, a person who writes a biography or an autobiography is producing a kind of literature that is written history. In this sense of the word, "history" signifies a type of literature different from empirical science, philosophy, and mathematics.

It is in this second sense of the word "history" that one can speak of historical research, of the methods of history, and of historical data.

The philosophy of history addresses itself to history as it occurs in reality. It is not concerned with the branch of literature that is called history.

Philosophies of history may take opposite points of view about the reality of history, one being that history is cyclical and repeats itself over and over again, the other being that history is progressive and involves nonrepetitive stages.

HONOR As people generally use the word "honor" they do not do so in the context of thinking about moral virtue. As a result they often confuse honor with fame.

A virtuous person is an honorable person, a person who ought to be honored by the community in which he or she lives. But the virtuous person does not seek honor, being secure in his or her own self-respect. Lack of honor does not detract from the efficacy of moral virtue as an operative factor in the pursuit of happiness—as a means to leading a good human life.

Virtuous persons may be considered fortunate if their virtue is recognized and publicly applauded. Being honored for one's virtue is a gift of good fortune, and like other gifts of fortune, not being honored is not a major obstacle to living well, as are poverty, loss of liberty, or loss of health.

These other goods of fortune are rightly desired by virtuous persons who recognize them as goods not entirely within their own power to achieve, as moral virtue itself is. Although this statement is true of honor also, virtuous persons may enjoy being honored while they are still alive instead of after they are dead; but they are under no moral obligation to seek it. They may think themselves dishonored if other persons do not give them the respect that accords with their own self-respect.

The public distribution of honors (as for example in the Queen's list in England) is thought to be one of the chief problems in distributive justice. For those who hold that honor and fame are distinct in principle, justice does not require fame to be proportionate to the possession of moral virtue.

Persons lacking moral virtue can achieve fame as readily as, or perhaps more easily than, those who have a high degree of moral virtue. Fame belongs to the great, the outstanding, the exceptional, without regard to their virtue or vice. Infamy is fame no less than good repute. The great scoundrel can be as famous as the great hero. There can be famous villains as well as famous saints. Existing in the reputation a person has, regardless of his or her accomplishments, fame does not tarnish as honor does when it is unmerited.

We normally desire the esteem of our fellow human beings, but is not this wish for the esteem of others a desire for fame rather than for honor? Virtuous persons will not seek fame or be unhappy for lack of it, for fame can be enjoyed by bad men and women, as well as good. When it is enjoyed by virtuous persons without being sought by them, it is not distinguishable from honor, for then it is deserved.

In a constitutional government, those who hold public office exercise more power than ordinary citizens who are not elected or appointed to administer government. But such power is vested in the political offices they hold, as defined by the Constitution, not in them personally. It is only personal power over others, competed for in worldly ventures, which is an object of wrong desire, and one which no virtuous person would seek. Machiavelli's *Prince* sets forth the rules by which this kind of wrong desire may be realized.

HUMAN NATURE AND NURTURE The French existentialist Merleau-Ponty summarizes the main point of nihilistic existentialism in the statement that "it is the nature of man not to have a nature." This denial of human nature, the same for all members of the human species, is so crucial to moral and political philosophy that we must point out the error made by the existentialists and also by a great many social scientists who also confuse nurture with nature.

Those who make this error would readily concede that in animals other than man, the individual members of a given taxonomic group do have a specific nature, genetically determined. They recognize that all lions and tigers, all whales and porpoises, behave in the same way.

Their genetically determined modes of behavior, which are the same in all members of a given species, constitute the properties of their specific nature. But it is maintained also that members of the human species do not have genetically determined behavioral dispositions that can be regarded as properties of a specific human nature.

Those who hold this view are quite correct in thinking that genetically determined human nature is different from the genetically determined specific natures of other animals. In a global investigation, one would find that the behavioral dispositions of human beings are as various as the places where we find human beings in action.

The reason is that specific human nature is constituted only by the possession at birth of the same *potentialities* for behavior rather than, as in other animals, the same actual behavioral dispositions.

Potentialities are capable of a wide range of actualizations. Take, for example, the capacity that all human beings have for acquiring language, and think of the innumerable languages that human beings do, in fact, acquire. An infant whose parents are French, taken at birth and brought up in a Swedish household, will learn to speak Swedish. That infant shares with every other infant, regardless of biological paternity, the same behavioral potentialities that can be actualized differently when the child is reared in a household that is different from the family in which it was born. One property of specific human nature is the potentiality for learning to speak a human language. The language that the child learns to speak is determined not by its specific nature, but by the way in which it is nurtured.

It is nurture that determines the different actualization of all the potentialities that constitute specific human nature. As they are nurtured differently, human beings actually behave differently at different times and places. But they all have at birth the same behavioral potentialities, and these potentialities constitute the specific nature of the human being.

IDEA   This is such an important word in the philosophical vocabulary that I have to repeat here some of the things in the entry on Cognition.

In the ancient world it was Plato, not Aristotle, who used the word "ideas" to signify intelligible objects of the understanding. He was correct in regarding ideas as intelligible objects, but incorrect in asserting that ideas exist in reality in addition to existing for the human mind as objects of conceptual thought.

On this point, Aristotle corrected Plato's error by using the word "concept" for the mental content that intends or signifies ideas as intentional objects. It was Aristotle and, after him, Aquinas who explicitly distinguished between *that which* the intellect understands and *that by which* it achieves such understanding.

This distinction between the *id quod* (that which) and the *id quo* (that by which) of our intellectual acts prevents us from ever saying that our concepts are *that which* we are conscious or aware of when we understand ideas. We could not be aware of the concepts in our minds and also *at the same time* be aware of their intelligible objects. If we were, we could not distinguish between them, which would mean we could not affirm that such objects exist and are shared by other minds.

This Aristotelian and Thomistic distinction between the *id quod* and the *id quo* of our intellectual acts of understanding has been completely lost in the modern world, beginning with Thomas Hobbes and Descartes, and especially with the nominalism of Bishop George Berkeley, David Hume, and John Locke.

The tradition of British empirical psychology and also of German and French psychology, used the word "ideas" for what were not ideas at all. In that modern tradition down to the present day, the word "idea" signifies the sensory content of the human mind—its sensations, perceptions, memories, and images. All this sensory content was treated as that which we are conscious of when we are engaged in thought.

This understanding raised the insoluble problem of how there could possibly be real existences as objects of thought. A vain attempt to solve this problem consisted of regarding the sensory contents in our minds as representations of real existences.

If they cannot be so regarded, the next step is complete skepticism. If the sensory contents of our minds, our so-called ideas, could not be regarded as representations of reality, then we could have no contact with a reality that is independent of our minds.

Kant, failing to correct Hume's errors, affirmed real existences, *things in themselves,* but also asserted that they are unknowable by us. From that time on in the modern world, the greatest of all modern philosophical mistakes was generated—the error of idealism, denying that there is any knowable reality independent of our mind. No ancient or medieval philosopher was an idealist in this sense of the word.

Finally, Berkeley and Hume were nominalists. They denied the existence of what they called "abstract ideas." All the common nouns in the vocabulary of everyday speech have general significance, referring to things that are the same in kind. Berkeley and Hume tried to explain how this was possible in the absence of any intellectual content in the human mind—in the absence of any acts of conceptual thought and of abstract ideas as intelligible objects.

In doing so, the nominalists contradicted themselves without being aware of it. Nominalism must be rejected as self-contradictory. (*See* the entries under Classes, Kinds and under Nominalism.)

IMMORTALITY This word has widely varied meanings when it is used to designate things that people regard as not destined to pass away. They think of a person's fame as immortal if it endures forever. They think of various institutions as immortal if their endurance is unending in time. But then they are not thinking philosophically, or they are not thinking of personal immortality as an article of faith in the three great religions of the West—Judaism, Christianity, and Islam.

The schoolbook syllogism "Socrates is a man, all men are mortal, Socrates is mortal" asserts that, as a matter of observable fact, Socrates is not immortal. The affirmation that the soul is immortal is an article of faith. It is not provable by reason.

It is sometimes said that the existence of God, the immortality of the soul, and the freedom of the will are all articles of faith. But the immortality of the soul differs from the existence of God and the freedom of the will. The latter two are in the sphere of reason. They are provable by reason in purely philosophical theology. But unlike the existence of God and free will, the immortality of the human soul is not within the province of philosophical theology. It is entirely in the sphere of religious faith.

In purely philosophical theology, all that can be affirmed by human reason is that the human intellect, being immaterial, is capable of subsisting after the death of the body. But the intellect's capacity for existing apart from the mortal body requires divine intervention to assure it of imperishable existence, either in heaven or in hell. (*See* the entry under Heaven and Hell.)

INFINITY The mathematical meaning of the word "infinity" is so well known that there is a tendency to overlook or neglect its metaphysical meaning; but it is the latter that is of prime importance in philosophical theology. Among the negative attributes of the supreme being is God's infinity. The supreme being is not only eternal (nontemporal) and immaterial, but also infinite.

In mathematics, we deal with potential infinities. For example, the series of whole numbers is endless. To any integer, no matter how large, another integer can be added. Between any two whole numbers is an infinite series of fractions. There is no pair of fractions so small that smaller fractions cannot be found. This potential infinite is the infinitesimal. To call these two infinities potential is to say that addition or division can go on endlessly. There is no *actually infinite* number.

When we say of the supreme being that God is *actually infinite,* as no physical thing is, not even the whole physical cosmos, we have a quite different meaning of the word "infinite" in mind. A thing differs in kind from things of another kind. Each belongs to a class that excludes other classes. Each lacks the traits that differentiate it from other individuals within the class of which both are members.

The finiteness of all the things of the physical cosmos is revealed by the traits or properties that it lacks. But the supreme being is unique. There is *only one supreme being.* God is not the member of any class that excludes other classes; and God is not an individual differing from other individuals, all of which are members of a given class. That is what we mean when we say God is not finite. His existence is unlimited.

JUSTICE AND EXPEDIENCY Only Aristotle uses the word "justice" in two radically different senses. He distinguishes between general and special justice. By justice in general he means justice as one of the four cardinal aspects of virtue, the other three being courage, temperance, and prudence. The morally virtuous man is a just man, and as such he is a temperate man and one who is also courageous and prudent.

By special justice, Aristotle means fairness in exchange and fairness in the distribution of goods. Fairness in exchange is commutative justice; and the other aspect of fairness is distributive justice.

Fairness is the special justice that is to be found in just laws; and it is in connection with the justice of human-made or positive law that Aristotle introduces the notion of equitable dispensation from a strict application of law to difficult cases. In the Anglo-American tradition of the common law, courts of chancery and equity provide such dispensations by the Lord Chancellor in Great Britain and by a similar official in some United States jurisdictions.

Machiavelli tells us that the prince should be just in the use of power, but if a just use of his power is not expedient, then he should be expedient in his effort to be a successful prince. The ideal use of power occurs when ruling justly is also expedient. But when that is not possible, Machiavelli says, then the prince or anyone else with ruling power must be unscrupulous and use whatever means will succeed in getting or keeping power even if the means employed are unjust.

KNOWLEDGE To have knowledge consists in possessing the truth. False knowledge is impossible. One cannot say "I know" and add "but what I know is false or incorrect."

There are two modes of truth—theoretical and practical. Theoretical truth is descriptive truth. We have such truth when our judgments conform to reality—a reality that is independent of our minds. We have practical truth when our judgments about what should be sought or what should be done conform to right desire.

The dichotomy of true and false is exhaustive only when we suspend judgment and entertain a proposition without making judgments. Our judgments may be probable or improbable. They have certitude only when they are beyond the shadow of doubt. Otherwise they are highly probable when they are beyond reasonable doubt; they have a lower degree of probability when, at a given time, they are supported by reasons and evidence that merely tip the scales in their favor.

The major divisions in the field of knowledge are (1) common-sense knowledge, (2) the knowledge obtained by scientific and historical research, and (3) the knowledge of reality that is philosophical—knowledge that is metaphysical or moral, knowledge obtained without research and investigation, by means of rational reflection on common sense and common experience.

Like philosophical knowledge, mathematics results from armchair thinking. But the objects of mathematical thought are not matters of fact. Mathematical truth is not factual truth.

I am inclined to say that the mathematician has a clear and coherent understanding of the objects with which mathematics deals, or lacks such understanding. The judgments of the mathematician are either true or false, correct or incorrect, clear or unclear. They are never more or less probable. Mathematical problems are either solvable with certitude, or they are undecidable.

There are two dimensions in which the philosopher does not have metaphysical or moral knowledge, but rather philosophical understanding. One is the consideration of ideas as intelligible objects. We should never say that philosophers *know* such objects as truth, good and evil, and beauty, but rather that they understand these intelligible objects—these objects of thought.

That understanding may be clear or unclear, adequate or inadequate, but it is never true or false. In addition to the understanding of intelligible objects, philosophers may have clear and adequate understanding of various intellectual disciplines, such as the philosophy of mathematics, the philosophy of science, and the philosophy of history.

This distinction between knowledge and understanding conforms to Aristotle's analysis of the intellectual virtues. What we have called knowledge he treats as science, distinguishing it from understanding and wisdom, which is the understanding of first principles and final ends.

LABOR The only difficulty about the word "labor" lies in the ambiguity of the word "work." Everyone understands that when we talk about laborers, we are referring to those who work for a living. Lacking property in the means of production (i.e., capital), they are reduced to toiling for the wages or salaries that they receive for their work.

If high-salaried executives have no source of income other than their salaries, and if they would not work unless they were paid for what they do, they, too, are toilers, similar to the least skilled workers who would not be working except for the extrinsic compensation they receive for what they are engaged in doing. Strictly speaking, in Marxist terms, they all belong to the proletariat—the toilers who would not work if they did not need the wages or salaries they receive.

Toil has no intrinsic value for those who do it, unless it be the avoidance of stealing as a way of obtaining what they need in order to survive. But there is another meaning of the word "work" that is not toil. Let us call toil subsistence-work. The other meaning of "work" is that which anyone would do if one did not need income for doing it, because it is work worth doing for its own sake and for its intrinsic value.

For example, composing music, painting a portrait, teaching any activity that perfects the individual who does it by improving or perfecting himself or herself, may be as tiring as toil, but we are willing to do such work because of the benefits it confers upon us or upon society. Let us call such work leisure-work. It is leisure-work even when it is compensated as well as when it is done without any thought of extrinsic compensation.

I would not use the words "human capital" for any member of the working class. In my view, the opposition of labor and capital must preserve the distinction between labor and all means of production and all consumable goods and services. Capital can be owned, but labor cannot be, except by the laborer himself or herself. Chattel slavery is a violation of this basic truth.

Unfortunately, the word "leisure" is generally misused as if it were a synonym for time that is free from subsistence-work, from leisure-work, and from other things that are needed to stay alive and healthy.

It is also used as if it referred to recreation or play. (*See* the entry under Leisure.) Leisuring is an activity as much as toiling is.

If we remember that there are two forms of work—toiling or subsistence-work and leisure-work—we will never again use the word "leisure" for recreations that comprise all the forms of playing, or for just doing nothing.

LANGUAGE In using the word "language," we have in mind the human languages that are both natural and conventional, such as English, French, German, and Swedish. They are natural in the sense that human beings are born with the potentiality of speaking and of learning them; they are conventional in the sense that the different societies in which human beings are nurtured determine the languages they learn and speak.

In addition to these natural languages, there are the special languages that human beings devise or invent, such as the language of a musical or choreographic score and the language of the visual arts. These are nonverbal languages, and the meaningful notations in them should be called symbols rather than signs.

Consider the language of music. What do the nonverbal symbols of a musical score mean? The notes on the page of a musical score designate the sounds to be played on various instruments or the sounds to be heard by anyone who can read the score.

This distinction calls our attention to the difference between designative signs (names in a verbal language) or symbols in a nonverbal language, such as music. But there is another dimension of significance. In addition to designative or naming significance, there are signs or symbols that function as signals.

For example, certain clouds in the sky mean the probability of rain; seeing smoke in the sky signals an unseen fire. These natural sequences are understood by us to have the significance of signals. When we use words rather than symbols, the "cry of fire" in a theatre signals an unseen combustion. When the cook at a lumber camp shouts from the porch, "Eats, come and get it," that verbal speech functions as a signal, not a designator. The natural cries of animals signal the behavior that other animals can expect to come from them or are warned to adopt themselves.

Only human beings have natural languages with designative or naming signs that signify the objects of conceptual as opposed to perceptual thought; thus only human beings have a syntactical language. In the laboratory, other animals that live in the world of perceptual thought can be trained to learn the meaning of a small vocabulary of designative signs. In the wild, without human intervention, other animals do not communicate with one another by means of any designative signs, but only by signaling.

The human infant learns a natural language in two ways. One is by learning the meaning of words that name or designate perceptually present objects. The other is by verbal description. When a child hears the word "kindergarten" for the first time, he or she may ask, "What is kindergarten?" He or she learns the meaning of that word by being told that a kindergarten is a place where little children go and learn to play with one another.

This is the ground for saying that only human beings have a verbal language that enables them to communicate with each other not only about the objects of perceptual and conceptual thought but also about objects that cannot be perceived or imagined, such as truth, goodness, and beauty; liberty, equality, and justice.

LAW The word "law" in the vocabulary of religious Jews, Christians, and Muslims means the Divinely ordained law of the Ten Commandments, and the Mosaic law enunciated in the last three books of the Pentateuch.

In the first two of these three religions, the Ten Commandments are laws individuals are obliged to observe and honor.

But for Christians, both Catholic and Protestant, what Jesus Christ called the two precepts of charity replace the Mosaic law. The two precepts of charity are to love God with all thy heart and all thy soul, and thy neighbor as thyself. On these two precepts, Christ tells us, "hang the law and the prophets." For Muslims, however, the Koran is a book of laws that deal with the everyday conduct of the faithful.

The law that is taught in our law schools is the human-made or positive law of the various jurisdictions, and also the underlying law of the U. S. Constitution, which all federal officeholders swear to uphold and all citizens regard as the fundamental safeguard of their natural rights.

The thing that connects the Constitution of the United States to the human-made laws of the federal government and of the fifty state jurisdictions is the natural law. Religious persons believe that the natural law is instilled in our minds and hearts by God, but even atheists can appeal to the natural law as the law of reason concerning what ought and ought not to be sought and what ought and ought not to be done.

It is the law of reason that proclaims our natural rights. Natural rights are the same at all times and places, but in the course of history there has been a growing recognition of such rights.

Chattel slavery was always a violation of man's natural right to liberty, but this natural right was not always recognized by most countries, and it is still far from being universally observed.

In the United States today there is still dispute between those who advocate a strict interpretation of the Constitution and those who think that reason can instruct us with regard to rights not mentioned in the Constitution or its Bill of Rights.

The strict constitutionalists have difficulty in explaining our government's foreign policy—one that condemns those nations in the world which do not respect the natural rights of human beings. Strict constitutionalists have difficulty also in recognizing that if chattel slavery is wrong now, it was wrong when it was incorporated into the Constitution originally, which was thus itself to that extent wrong, and made right only with the Thirteenth, Fourteenth, and Fifteenth Amendments.

If I am correct in thinking that every human being has a right to a decent livelihood, then it must be inferred that the United States has not yet become a nation that secures all the natural rights of its citizens. It may not succeed in doing so until late in the next century.

LEISURE *See* the entry under Labor.

In 1926, the American economist Thorstein Veblen wrote *The Theory of the Leisure Class: An Economic Study of Institutions*. It should have been entitled *The Lives of the Idle Rich*.

Veblen egregiously misused the word "leisure" for idleness and recreational activities, the sports and games at which the idle rich played when they were not engaged competitively in what Veblen called "conspicuous consumption" of clothing, jewelry, and real estate.

Not having to toil for a living, and not being given to the often exhausting details of real leisure-work, they had ample free time to disport themselves or be bored. Veblen also misused the word "leisure" for time that is free, not for an activity like work that consumes time usefully, even when it is not compensated at all.

The English word "leisure" derives from the Latin *licēre,* which means an activity that is permissible. This meaning runs counter to the understanding that leisure-work is not only permissible but also morally obligatory for anyone trying to live a morally good life.

The English word "leisure" also translates the Greek word *scholē* as "school" and stands for an activity that involves learning or self-improvement.

When this meaning is fully understood, the mistake will never be made of using "leisure" to denote "free time" or regarding leisuring as a synonym for playing and recreation.

LIBERAL ARTS As currently used by the educational establishment, the phrase "liberal arts" applies to any academic program that offers a course of study that is not strictly vocational.

That is not what the phrase "liberal arts" referred to in antiquity and the Middle Ages. In Plato's *Republic,* where the education of the guardians is considered, the seven liberal arts are first mentioned.

They are the verbal arts of the trivium and the mathematical arts of the quadrivium. The three arts of the trivium are the arts of grammar, logic, and rhetoric. The four arts of the quadrivium are the arts of arithmetic, geometry, music, and astronomy. Taken together, the seven arts were understood to provide the skills required to deal with works in what we now call the humanities and with works in mathematics and in what we now call the sciences.

In the universities of the twelfth and thirteenth centuries the Bachelor of Arts degree was conferred on those who had completed their initiation into the arts of the trivium. Their teachers were masters of these arts; and having an M.A. degree was the highest academic attainment. There was no Ph.D. degree; that was an invention of the German universities in the nineteenth century. The three higher faculties were the faculties of medicine, law, and theology.

I have reworded the arts of the trivium as the skills of reading and writing, of speaking and listening, of reasoning and of persuading. In my account of the Paideia reform of public schooling in the United States, I have advocated the coaching of these fundamental skills as requisite for all students. They are skills that all initiates should possess when they graduate from secondary school and should be awarded the B.A. degree.

To become masters of these arts may take the better part of a lifetime, not only in so-called liberal colleges but also in the years of maturity. If our colleges are to be places of liberal learning, there should be no training for specific jobs that involve earning a living. Specific job training should be given only to those not going to college, but who, after receiving their B.A. degree, spend time in vocational training that is offered by community colleges.

In our universities, there should also be instruction in purely liberal programs that may include the preparation of teachers and preparation for the learned professions.

LIBERTY The word "liberty" and the word "freedom" are strictly synonymous and interchangeable. The word "freedom" carries an adjective that can be used as a modifier. The word "liberty" does not lend itself to such usage.

The Institute for Philosophical Research spent ten years studying the idea of freedom, and published two large volumes on the subject. Liberty is also one of the six great ideas that we studied.

The word "freedom" and with it the word "liberty" cover four major modalities of freedom. These had to be carefully identified in order to discover the authors who discussed and disputed freedom in one or more of these four modalities. In the Institute's work, we discovered two ways in which to identify these modalities of the subject.

The first involved identifying how the freedom or liberty is possessed, either naturally, by acquisition, or circumstantially. Thus, for example, human beings have the freedom of a free will either as a natural endowment, or they do not have it at all. They have the moral freedom or liberty of being able to will as they ought as a consequence of moral virtue on their part; and their freedom to act as they please derives from the favorable circumstances under which they live.

The second method of identifying the four freedoms involved a statement about what natural, acquired, and circumstantial freedoms consist in. In the case of natural freedom, it was free choice—the ability to choose otherwise in every act of free will. We have already seen that moral liberty is the ability to will as one ought to will; and circumstantial freedom is the freedom to do as we please.

We called the circumstantial freedom the freedom of self-realization; the moral liberty, the acquired freedom of self-perfection; and the natural freedom, the freedom of self-determination.

That left only one other freedom to identify, one that really is an aspect of circumstantial freedom; namely, political liberty. A people have political liberty under favorable circumstances when they are governed with their own consent and with a voice in their government.

These four modalities of freedom or liberty do not involve an equivocal use of those words, for we were able to show a thread that ties them all together. That thread of meaning can be expressed in the statement that what is common to all four modalities (or certainly the major three, if not that aspect of circumstantial freedom which is political liberty) lies in the power of the self to be dominant.

LOVE The word that we must examine in thinking about love is "desire." There are two modes of desire, acquisitive and benevolent, desire that leads to getting and desire that leads to giving. The word "love" is misused if it is used for acquisitive desire and, in that connection, carries the connotation of sexual desire.

Imagine a human world from which gender and sex were totally absent but everything else remained the same. If you say that you cannot imagine such a world, I must respond by saying that you do not understand the meaning of the word "love." Certainly in such a world, one would love one's country, one would love the friends one admired, and one would love God and understand what it means to say that God is love.

The Greeks and Romans had three words for the three kinds of love, whereas in English we use the one word "love" for all three kinds. In Greek, the words are *eros, philia,* and *agapē*. In Latin the words are *amor, amacitia,* and *caritas*.

It is only erotic or amorous love that involves sexual desire and activity, but even erotic love is benevolent in its concern for the enjoyment of sex by the loved one. Sexual activity devoid of benevolent impulse is not love but lust, and lust, like greed, is a mortal sin.

Love is always altruistic, not selfish. Only children and childish persons ever misuse the word "love" for selfish desire, saying "I love candy" or "I love popcorn."

Love is more altruistic than justice. Justice is primarily negative, its precept being not to judge or harm others. But love is entirely positive in its precepts. Aristotle tells us that if all human beings were friends, justice would not be necessary, for if they loved those whom they thought admirable, they would be benevolently disposed toward them.

MACHINE   Of all the things in the universe, those which are most intelligible, not in themselves but to us, are the machines that we ourselves contrive and produce. We understand them better than we understand ourselves or any living organism that is besouled or animated.

In the twentieth century, the century in which the computer has had such extraordinary development, machines have taken on a new fascination for human beings, especially the artificial-intelligence machines for which extravagant claims have been made—claims that machines can think, claims that they can do whatever the human mind can do and do it faster and better.

There is no question that artificial intelligence or AI machines can perform all mathematical and logical operations; but the human mind does not think logically but in some other fashion that the machine cannot replicate.

The distinctively human mind, as opposed to the animal mind, has intellectual power. If the intellect itself is an immaterial power, then, of course, no machines can perform intellectual operations, for machines are entirely material contraptions.

It was Alan Turing who proposed a test for solving the problem of whether machines can think in the way that human beings do. If, behind a screen, there is a machine to be interrogated by a human being standing before the screen, and if the human interrogator cannot tell whether his questions are being answered by another human being or by a machine, then the machine succeeds in passing the Turing test.

The Turing test is really the test that René Descartes proposed when, having declared that matter cannot think, he said that no machine can engage in conversation with a human being.

Computers, even the most sophisticated of them, have to be programmed. This stricture also applies to AI machines. But if a conversation between two human beings were to go on endlessly or, what is the same in effect, for a very long time, it would take unpredictable turns that could not be programmed. That is why the AI machine may never succeed in being undetectable when it takes the Turing test.

Purely logical thinking is the kind of thinking which is mechanical and which a machine can do. But human beings think by intuitive leaps and then use logic to demonstrate the conclusions that are reached without any logical process whatsoever.

MAN When we use the word "man" not for the male gender or male member of the human species, but for all members of the species, then we must take a position that answers these questions:

1. Is man different in kind or only in degree from animals, especially other mammals?
2. If different in kind, not in degree, is that difference superficial and therefore reducible to a difference in degree, or is it radical and irreducible?

Two entities differ in degree if both have the same defining traits, but one has more and one has less of the same trait.

A superficial difference in kind between two things becomes a difference in degree by further analysis of the difference between them. Then the superficial difference in kind will be only an apparent, not a real, difference in kind.

Consider, for example, the three states of matter: the solid as opposed to the liquid and the gaseous state. In its solid state, water can be walked on, but not in its liquid state. This would appear to be a difference in kind between the solid state of matter and the liquid state. But when we discover that these two states of matter are reducible to the velocity at which the molecules of water and of ice are in motion, we learn that the difference in kind between water and ice is only a difference in the degree of the velocity of molecular particles. It is only superficially a difference in kind and it is really reducible to a difference in degree.

The same applies to the superficial difference in kind between matter in its liquid state and matter in its gaseous state. It appears to be a difference in kind: we can take a cupful of water, but we cannot take a cupful of air.

When the difference in kind cannot thus be reduced to a difference in degree, it remains a difference in kind. The intellectual human mind has properties that cannot be reduced to a difference in degree from the minds of other mammals. The difference in kind is radical, not superficial, real, not apparent.

To claim that the difference between the human mind and the minds of other mammals is a radical difference in kind is to claim that the human mind has intellectual powers that animal minds do not have at all. Other mammals' minds can be explained in material terms, whereas the human mind's intellectual power cannot be. This is not to deny that we share other mental powers with animals, who, like ourselves, operate in the world of perceptual thought—the world of things that are perceptually present, the world of sensation, imagination, and memory.

In addition, the human mind operates in the world of conceptual thought, where it deals with objects that are not perceptually present, nor can they ever be. This ability makes it radically different in kind.

MATTER The word "matter" has a totally different meaning in ancient and medieval philosophy from that which it has in modern physics.

In modern physics, its usual significance lies in such phrases as "matter and energy." In fact, matter is a form of energy and can be transformed into it by the formula $E = mc^2$, where c is the constant velocity of light. In quantum theory, especially in quantum electrodynamics (QED), matter obeys the laws of particle physics.

In Aristotelian philosophy, the word "matter" signifies potentiality. Pure potentiality, with no actuality, cannot exist. Existent matter, or what has been called signate matter, is formed of somewhat actualized potentiality. God is pure actuality because God is totally immaterial. The Greek word for form without matter, or pure actuality, is *energeia,* from which is derived the English word "energy."

In everyday speech, the word "matter" is usually used to designate what physical things are made of. The material cause in artistic production is the matter transformed. The formal cause is the form in the artist's mind, which he or she uses when attempting to transform the matter by shaping it one way or another. In other words, the material cause is signate matter—a potentiality already actualized and thus limited—that the artist transforms by actualizing the limited potentialities of the matter.

In the process of eating, involving ingestion, digestion, and assimilation, the matter involved is a definite potentiality that is actualized in the process of assimilation by becoming actually like the body of the person who eats the food.

In the process of reproduction, the genetic code contained in the DNA molecule determines all the inherited potentialities of the offspring's body. These are actualized in the process of growth and development.

If I am correct in my theory of the immateriality of the human intellect, it is an actuality rather than a potentiality, and so cannot be genetically determined. Yet intellectual capacities seem to be inherited. This is a mystery.

MEDICINE   In the long history of medicine, from Hippocrates and Galen down to the present, the word "medicine" signifies both an art and a science, and also the therapeutic substances that physicians prescribe for their patients.

Prescribed medicine or drugs act therapeutically on the body of the patient. They are less violent than surgery, but like surgery, they are remedies that the physician should resort to only if the malady cannot be treated by the physician working with the body's own process of maintaining or regaining health.

In the view of Hippocrates, the healer is a cooperative, not an operative artist. If he prescribes drugs or surgery he is operative, but if he controls the diet, the air the patient breathes, and the places where the patient lives, he is, like the farmer and the teacher, a cooperative artist.

The body works to preserve its own health. In the ancient science of medicine, a healthy organism was one in which there was a balance of the bodily humors.

In our day, technologically advanced therapy is highly specialized. It does not treat the human being as a whole nor does it consider the social and physical environment in which the ill person lives. What is sometimes called alternative therapy is a return to the Hippocratic view of medicine as a cooperative, not an operative art.

MEMORY AND IMAGINATION Along with perception, memory and imagination name the main sensitive powers. Many of our memories are verbal and implement all the processes of thought, both perceptual and conceptual thought.

When our memories are not verbal, that which we remember recalls past events or occasions. The past, which no longer exists, becomes present to us in recollection. We actually have a nonexistent past present to us in our minds.

Imagination also presents to our minds objects that do not actually exist. It is the power by which we explore the realm of the possible. When our senses cooperate with our intellects and we are not conceptually blind, we can imagine objects which may exist at some future time, or which are merely figments or fictions of our imagination. They are intelligible to us, even though we understand them as constructed by us, such as mermaids and centaurs.

The intellectual imagination enriches human experience by giving us the power to deal with objects that are not accessible to other animals. The world in which animals live is limited to that which is perceptually present or remembered.

The characters in narrative fiction are our own imaginative constructs. Julius Caesar, for example, as described in Plutarch's *Lives,* can be remembered by us, but Julius Caesar, a character in a play by Shakespeare, is our own imaginative construct. It exists only in our imagination. It is a mental fiction.

Verbal memories do not persist for long periods. They are soon forgotten, though they can be revived. There is no purely intellectual memory. Instead the intellect forms habits. When we have the habit of understanding it retains what, at an earlier time, we understood. This habit of understanding is strengthened and reinforced by exercising the habit.

METAPHYSICS "Metaphysics" is a word that Aristotle's editors invented to name books he wrote that came after his books on physics. These later books deal with the modes of being or existence, with the reality that is independent of our minds and is immaterial or nonphysical. Unlike mathematics, metaphysics does not deal with ideal objects abstracted from the realm of physical things. It deals with the immaterial, such as God and the human intellect. Aristotle sometimes refers to it as theology and today we would call it philosophical theology.

In the nineteenth century something called positivism arose in the writings of Auguste Comte. For him, only the positive empirical sciences give us knowledge of reality. For him, religion and philosophy were the gibberish of a bygone era.

Positivism was further developed in the twentieth century by the Viennese circle of antimetaphysical authors. It later became the position known as "logical positivism." Without any understanding of what was meant by calling the book *Metaphysics,* the logical positivists dismissed metaphysical discussion as a misuse of language.

Today, another exclusively modern error stands in the way of reviving what Aristotle treated as a valid branch of philosophical thought. It is the error of ontological idealism—the denial of any reality independent of our minds. This position, of course, invalidates philosophy itself as a first-order discipline.

NOMINALISM The word "nominalism" refers to a serious error that occurred in modern philosophy, especially in the writings of Bishop George Berkeley and David Hume. It is an error in philosophical psychology.

Both Berkeley and Hume think that man is equipped with sensitive faculties only. They assume that man has no intellect, or they deny its existence. The problem they faced was explaining the meaning of the general words in our everyday language; for example, the common nouns that signify classes or kinds.

If human beings enjoyed the power of conceptual, as opposed to perceptual thought, there would be no difficulty in explaining how words signify generalities or universals. They would derive their significance from concepts that give us our understanding of classes or kinds.

But regarding human beings as deprived of conceptual thought poses a problem for Berkeley and Hume. They are compelled to say that when we use words that appear to have general significance, we are applying them to a number of perceived individuals *indifferently;* that is, without any difference in the meaning of the word thus applied. This amounts to saying that there is a certain sameness in the individual things that the speaker or writer recognizes.

Are they not contradicting themselves when they offer this explanation of the meaning of general terms or common nouns? If human beings do not have conceptual thought, how can they recognize the sameness that permits the nominalists to say that the same word can be applied *indifferently* to a number of individuals?

Are they not contradicting themselves? Should not nominalism—the assertion that names have general significance even though human beings can have no understanding of kinds or classes—be rejected?

OBJECTIVE AND SUBJECTIVE These two words are used in the everyday speech of almost everyone, but not with the philosophical significance they should have.

When, speaking or writing philosophically, we declare that something is objective, we are saying that it is the same for all individuals.

That being so, it is public, not private. It can be a common object about which two or more individuals may engage in conversation, agree or disagree, and dispute with each other.

But when we declare that something is subjective, we are saying that it is different for you, for me, and for many other individuals. It belongs in the realm of the private. It is not a public matter that can be discussed with the aim of arriving at a shared understanding of it.

In the twentieth century, the statement that all value judgments are subjective means, in effect, that value judgments—about what is good or bad, right or wrong—are matters of personal prejudice or private opinion. They are not objectively true or false, and so moral philosophy is dismissed as being noncognitive. Our judgments of matters of fact are genuine knowledge, but not our value judgments.

153

OPINION The word "opinion" is in the same family of words to which "knowledge" belongs. Both words refer to acts of the mind that can be objectively true or false. But there is an important difference. False knowledge is self-contradictory. If a statement is false it does not express our knowledge. But a statement of opinion can be either true or false.

To take account of this difference between knowledge and opinion, it is necessary to regard opinions as only probably true or false, whereas knowledge is true beyond the shadow of a doubt. It has certitude. Self-evident truths, truths the opposites of which are unthinkable, are invariant truths. Moreover, those things which can be validly deduced from such truths are similarly beyond the shadow of a doubt. They have certitude.

The Greek language had two words that we can translate into English by referring to the assurance we have about their truth. One was the word *epistēmē*. The other was the word *doxa*.

Epistēmē, from which we get the English word "epistemology," stands for truths that have invariable certitude for us. *Doxa* is the word from which we derive the word "orthodox." That English word means right opinion—opinion of which, at a given moment in time and in the light of all the then available evidence and reasons, we feel assured either beyond a reasonable doubt or at least by a preponderance of the then available evidence and reasons. But unlike knowledge in the strongest sense of that term (*epistēmē*), *doxa* is never beyond the shadow of a doubt; it includes all doubtable truths. The assurance we have about their truth is always determined, at a given time, by the character of the evidence and reasons we then have at our disposal.

Setting aside, for the moment, the very few propositions that are either self-evident or demonstrable in terms of valid deductions from self-evident truths, all the propositions of history, of the empirical sciences, and of philosophy fall in the sphere of doubt. They are all instances of *doxa*, not *epistēmē*.

It is only in the last few centuries of modern time that philosophers have bewildered themselves with the problems of epistemology. If they had concerned themselves with the opinions of historians, empirical scientists, and philosophers, their inquiries would have been much more fruitful.

PHILOSOPHY   Elsewhere I have distinguished philosophy from mathematics, from history, and from all the empirical sciences, by declaring philosophy to be a noninvestigative discipline that employs the evidence of common experience. Unlike history and the empirical sciences that employ the evidence of special experience discovered by their specifically investigative methods, philosophy is strictly armchair thinking.

But it may be said also that mathematics is armchair thinking. Like the philosopher, the mathematician does not have to leave the desk for a moment to carry on any investigations in order to engage in mathematical thought. But unlike the philosopher, the mathematician is not concerned with objects that have any existence in a reality independent of our minds.

This fourfold array of the disciplines—philosophy, mathematics, history, and the empirical sciences—distinguishes them from one another by their characteristically different methods. Questions that can be answered by one method cannot be answered by the other methods. Some questions may not be purely scientific or purely philosophical. But if a question is purely philosophical, then it is a question to which the methods of the other three disciplines cannot contribute.

This approach enables us to explain how, in modern times, when philosophy is dismissed by logical positivists as giving us no truths about an independent reality, the invidious dismissal of philosophy as mere opinion can be countered by showing the way in which there is progress in philosophy as well as in science, agreement in philosophy as well as in science, and a practical utility of philosophy as well as of science.

In every case, the progress, the agreements, and the use of philosophy will be characteristically different from that which occurs in the empirical sciences.

We are also enabled to deal with the history of philosophy, in ancient, medieval, and modern times, by reference not to the various doctrines espoused in these different epochs, but only by reference to the slow development of the method that is truly philosophical. This I call a purely procedural, not substantive, history of philosophy; and from this procedural point of view, philosophy has achieved its maturity only in recent years.

The four dimensions of philosophy are metaphysical, moral, objective, and categorical.

PLEASURE AND PAIN   There are two meanings of the word "pleasure," and only one of the word "pain"—words that are used by everyone in daily discourse without observing the difference in these meanings.

Pain is a sensation. In our bodies, there are peripheral and visceral nerve endings that, when stimulated, cause us to feel pain. Pleasure, in sharp distinction from pain, is not a sensation, though we feel it. We have no neurophysiological centers of pleasure.

The two meanings of pleasure refer to pleasures that we all feel. One is sensual pleasure, the pleasure that is an object of desire. Its bodily aspect is to be found in certain sensory stimulations, such as the pleasure we feel when we are thirsty on a hot day and are given a drink of cold liquid, the pleasure we feel when being tickled, the pleasure we feel when the tension of sexual desire is relieved by an orgasm.

These are all sensible and sensual pleasures that are objects of desire, even though there are no neurophysiological spots on or in our bodies that are nerve endings for pleasure as there are such stimulatory nerve endings for pain. The erogenous zones may be such physiological pleasure spots.

The other meaning of the word "pleasure" lies in the pleasure we feel when our desires are satisfied. It is the pleasure of contentment. We use the word "pleasure" in this way when we say that something we have done or something done to us pleases us.

This identification of pleasure with the satisfaction of desire gives another meaning to the word "pain" that has no basis in our nervous system. We often say we are pained when we mean that we are discontented or dissatisfied.

POETRY The word "poetry" is now generally used as if it referred to lyric poetry, a kind of writing that is not prose or prosaic. What is written in prose is always capable of being written in words other than the words used. But when something is written poetically, the words used are the *only* words adequate for expressing the writer's intent.

The opposition between verse and prose, or

between poetical and prosaic writing, is not relevant to what the word "poetry" meant in ancient and medieval times, and meant in modern times until the nineteenth century. Poetry was then understood to stand for all imaginative literature, for all narrative fiction—for novels and dramas, all works of the intellectual imagination.

Aristotle tells us in his *Poetics* that poetry is more philosophical than history, because historical narratives deal with singular past events, whereas poetical narratives deal with possible generalities. The characters in imaginative literature are types of human nature. This is unaffected by the style of writing, whether in verse or prose.

Another saying worth remembering here is that history is often stranger than fiction. What actually did happen in the past is less intelligible to us than what might have happened.

Finally, we must consider the distinction between poetical and logical truth. When we think that something is logically true, we must also think that what is contrary or contradictory to the proposition we judge to be true must be false. Logical truth is exclusionary. Not so for what is only poetically true, for here we are dealing with narratives that have verisimilitude—acceptable to us because they are likely to be true.

Poetical truth is not exclusionary. For example, among the Greek tragedies there can be many stories about Clytemnestra and Electra, all different but all poetically true.

PRIVATE PROPERTY Many people use the expression "private property" and even the word "mine" without being acquainted with John Locke's labor theory of property. They will find that theory stated with maximum clarity in Chapter V of his *Second Treatise Concerning Civil Government*.

Everyone, according to Locke, owns himself by right and the power invested in his mind and his hands. This is the simplest declaration of the fundamental injustice of chattel slavery, which is the ownership of one human being by another.

After this first step, Locke proceeds by distinguishing between the common and the proper. That which is not owned by anybody at all, yet may be used by all, are certain tracts of public land that the community makes available to all members and can be used by them in common.

The famous Boston Common is an example of this distinction.

Forgetting the existence of Indian tribes in the New World of America, Locke refers to a time when all the world was like America, given by God to all human beings in common for their invasion and exploitation. What any human being, invading this God-given common, appropriated to himself or herself by his own labor became his or her private property.

When a man, for example, caught and tamed a wild horse, that became his horse; when he fenced in a plot of land and cultivated it by using his horse to pull tools that he himself made by his own labor, the resulting produce and the land itself became his private properties.

Locke thinks that no one should appropriate more than he can store for a future day. Nothing should be wasted. Enough should be left in the common for others to appropriate.

In one passage Locke considers the possibility of the solitary farmer employing another person to work for him. Let us consider this more complicated situation. Let Brown be the solitary farmer who, standing at his fence, accosts Smith, a passing journeyman, with a sack of clothes and other possessions slung over his back.

Brown says to Smith, "If you will work for me during the next week, using my land, my horse, and my tools, I will give you a share of what is produced during the week." Smith voluntarily accepts these terms.

That next week, Brown does no work at all. He stays inside his cabin, reading or thinking. At the end of the week Brown pays Smith off to Smith's satisfaction, and Smith goes on his way. Brown keeps for himself that share of the produce which is left after Smith has been paid off.

The question to be answered is: Did Brown rightfully earn that share of the week's produce which he claims for himself after he has paid Smith off, even though he himself did not do a stroke of work during the week that Smith labored for him?

Locke's answer to that question is affirmative. The reason is that even though the wealth acquired by Brown was not the result of his own labor, it could not have been produced by his servant if Brown had not put his own productive property to work during that week.

In other words, Brown is a capitalist who earns wealth without himself laboring but at the same time putting his capital (i.e., the means of production) to work.

PROGRESS The word "progress" is a modern word. It was not used in the ancient and medieval world. But what the word signifies did have some bearing on the philosophy of history that developed in antiquity and in the Middle Ages.

In the ancient world, one view of the pattern of human history was that it was cyclical—an everlastingly recurrent pattern of growth and decline.

Another ancient view was that the golden age of mankind was in the far distant past. Since then there has been a steady decline.

In his *City of God,* Augustine tells us that divine providence operates in the opposite direction. Man's relation to God will have a brighter future.

For both Aristotle and Aquinas, no individual thinker contributes to improvements in thought —improvements in science and philosophy. By the collaboration of many, advances are made.

With regard to progress itself, as that is discussed in modern times, certain questions should be in everyone's mind. One is the question of whether there is any progress in human nature— whether in the course of historical time, human beings are improved in the traits that all human beings, as members of the same species, share.

Another basic question is whether such progress as has been achieved is entirely in human institutions. If so, the next question to be considered is whether this institutional progress is quantitative or meliorative—whether the institutional improvements are in the direction of more and more or in the direction of better and better.

The facts of history in the last 3,000 years, and certainly in the last 600, contain many examples of quantitative progress: the human population has increased in size; with advances in medicine, human beings live longer than they once did; and as scientific knowledge has grown from century to century, its technological applications have showered on us more and more instruments that have been immensely useful. In this century, there are more scientists alive and working together than in any previous period.

But the question remains whether the more is also the better—whether the progress is meliorative as well as quantitative. To answer this question, we must appeal to the fundamental principles of ethics for the standards of evaluation. (I recommend a book by Charles Van Doren entitled *The Idea of Progress* [New York:

Frederick A. Praeger, Publishers, 1967], especially Book Two, Part II, and Appendix, pp. 317–475.)

PUNISHMENT The word "punishment" is used in the criminal law to stand for whatever treatment the state recommends for convicted offenders. That treatment may be either utilitarian or retributive, but it cannot be both.

The treatment is retributive when the punishment fits the crime, not the criminal. Retributive punishment may or may not have a salutary effect upon the criminal, but the severity of the punishment must be measured by the seriousness of the crime. What was once called the "lex talionis" required a just proportion between the injury done to the victim of the crime and the injury to be suffered by the criminal—an eye for an eye, a life for a life.

Punishment is utilitarian or pragmatic when its aim is not to do strict justice, but rather to deter or reform criminals. Here the treatment accorded offenders judged guilty of committing the same offense may not be the same. The treatment may vary with the age and the character of the offender.

It is in this context that the question of capital punishment must be considered by those who think the aim of punishment should be to prevent crime, and particularly recidivism, which is the recurrent criminality of offenders who are paroled.

Some states have now abolished capital punishment on the grounds that it is unjust, a violation of the right to life. While the offender is alive, errors that may have occurred in his or her trial can be rectified. The right to life is not violated by the incarceration of the offender for life with no parole allowed. Nor is the right to liberty violated, for the offender incarcerated for life without parole still retains his right to liberty, even though his exercise of liberty is severely curtailed.

The offender's right to liberty would be violated only if the warden treated the incarcerated offender as his personal slave. That would be unjust because it would be a violation of the offender's right to be treated as a free human being rather than as a slave.

Current recommendations that criminals found

guilty of three offenses should be incarcerated for life with no parole allowed is not a violation of human rights. They do not deprive the repeated offender's life or liberty, but they may be pragmatically sound measures aimed at reducing recidivism and thus preventing crime.

REALITY AND APPEARANCE The word "reality" has had a special meaning in modern times since Immanuel Kant's so-called Copernican revolution in philosophy declared that the thing in itself—the *Ding an sich*—is not knowable by us.

It was Kant's Copernican revolution that introduced into philosophy the fundamental error of ontological idealism, an error not found in ancient and medieval thought. Before Kant, there were self-refuting skeptics, but no idealists. The word "reality" signified not only that which exists in complete independence of the human mind, but also that which is knowable by and intelligible to us.

The great philosophers of antiquity and of the Middle Ages were all realists. Aristotle and Aquinas, for example, asserted that we could know and understand a past that no longer existed, but was nevertheless an object of perceptual thought. That reality has existence for us. (*See* the entry under Cognition.)

It is in this context that the word "appearance" is used. It has different meanings for realists who naively assert that reality is exactly the same as it appears to be and those who assert more critically that what appears to us may not be identical in character with what really exists.

RELIGION The word "religion" has many meanings in popular speech. That is especially so if we consider how it is used globally for Western and Far Eastern religions. Only in the three Western religions (Judaism, Christianity, and Islam) and perhaps one religion in the Far East (Sikhism) are questions about truth raised. Only the three Western religions have sacred scriptures, each of which claims logical or factual truth for its credal doctrines and denies that the other two are as true as it is.

The Old Testament is affirmed as the revealed word of God by religious Christians and also by the religion of Islam; but the New Testament and the Koran are not accepted as revealed truth by the Jews, and the New Testament is not accepted as revealed truth by the religion of Islam.

When considering these three Western religions, all of which claim to be based on God's revelation of Himself, we must face the exclusionary character of logical truth. They cannot all be equally true. The question to be decided is which are more true than the others, and which are less true.

Only the three Western religions and one Far Eastern religion (the religion of the Sikhs) are monotheistic. Among the religions of the Far East, some are polytheistic and some are nontheistic. They are cosmological. Some are filled with myths that require interpretation, and some, especially Hinduism, claim only poetical truth and so do not exclude other religions.

With regard to the religions of the Far East, it is difficult to draw the line between religion and philosophy. Many of these religions, doctrinally considered, are expressions of purely human wisdom, though in them we find common vestiges of religious worship such as the separation of the sacred from the secular, a priesthood, holy men, and ceremonial practices such as fasting, prayer, sacrifices, and holy days.

The basic distinction to be remembered here is that between natural and supernatural knowledge. Natural knowledge, both sensitive and intellectual, is the knowledge we attain by the unaided exercise of our cognitive faculties. In sharp distinction is supernatural knowledge— the knowledge we receive by divine revelation.

What Christians declare when they recite the Nicene Creed is what they believe as articles of their religious faith. The presence or absence of supernatural knowledge is the critical point of difference between the revealed religions and purely philosophical wisdom. (*See* the entries under Belief and under Cognition.)

REPRESENTATION The question that this word raises concerns the obligations of persons chosen to represent the citizens whose votes send them to the legislature of a constitutional government, whether it be an oligarchy with limited suffrage or a democracy with universal suffrage.

When questions come before the legislative body of which they are members, should their response be determined by the view held by their constituents, or should they decide which side to take on an issue before the legislature in terms of their own judgment of what is the right solution of the problem, whether or not it concurs with the view held by their constituents?

Edmund Burke answered this question in his *Letter to the Sheriffs of Bristol,* whose representative he was. He said that if they had elected him because of his intellectual qualities, they should look upon him as better able than they to decide which side of the issue being debated in the legislature was the correct side to take. He did not regard himself as an envoy to act as instructed by them.

Today, most of our legislators are very attentive to opinion polls, as well as to the letters they receive from their constituents. If they are guided by these indications, they do not regard themselves as functioning in the way that Burke recommended.

Some compromise between these two positions is possible. It is sometimes thought that the phrase "government by the people" calls for participatory rather than representative democracy. But if the state or nation is large and populous, it is not feasible to conduct its affairs in the manner of a small-town meeting in which the citizens take a direct and active part in their own government. On the other hand, their wishes should not be despised. (I recommend to readers that they consult J. S. Mill's *Representative Government*. They will find in Chapter 12, which is entitled "Ought Pledges to Be Required from Members of Parliament?," Mill's views on the question dealt with by Edmund Burke.)

RIGHTS, NATURAL AND CIVIL The word "rights" is a basic word in the vocabulary of political science and political philosophy.

Civil or political rights are those included in constitutions or in bills of rights. They are the rights stated in the Constitution of the United States, its amendments, and particularly in the first ten amendments that are called our American Bill of Rights.

These rights are either granted or not granted by the state, and since they are within the power of the state to grant, they can be countermanded by the state when in the course of history fundamental changes in policy are contemplated.

The Ninth Amendment contains an implicit

reference to natural rights by declaring that "The enumeration in the Constitution of certain rights shall not be construed to deny or disparage others retained by the people." Jurists who deny the existence of natural rights think that this Ninth Amendment is an unfortunate blemish in our Constitution because it appears to be an affirmation of natural rights.

Why? Because in 1793, when this amendment was adopted, the other rights retained by the people were probably the natural rights mentioned in the second paragraph of the Declaration of Independence, such as the inalienable rights to life and liberty.

Natural rights are inherent in human nature. They are, therefore, inalienable and belong to every human being *with no exceptions*. They are specifically human rights. Now that they have become part of our government's declared foreign policy, it becomes self-contradictory for legal positivists to deny the existence of natural law and natural rights, and yet to subscribe to our government's foreign policy with regard to human rights.

The exponents and defenders of natural and human rights can argue that the existence of natural rights derives from the distinction between needs and wants—or, what is the same, between natural and acquired desires. Since human needs are the needs inherent in human nature, identified by the potentialities that define them, natural rights are rights to the real goods that everyone needs in order to live a morally good human life.

The statement in the Declaration of Independence that all human beings have certain inalienable rights can be expanded to say that these include the right to life, the right to liberty, and the right to whatever any human being needs in order to live humanly well.

Natural rights can be violated or secured by governments, but a perfectly just government is one that secures and safeguards all natural and human rights.

SCIENCE The word "science" has changed its meaning as we pass from antiquity and the Middle Ages to modern times, especially to the nineteenth and twentieth centuries.

Today it means the observational or investigative sciences, sometimes called the empirical and experimental sciences. It must be added that the word "science" is also used to refer to mathematics, which is clearly nonempirical and noninvestigative.

The adjective "scientific" is used as a term of praise conferred on other disciplines; such disciplines employ methods which have a certain objectivity in their appeal to evidence which sets them apart from mere, unfounded opinion. Though history is not a science, nor is philosophy, nevertheless as branches of humanistic scholarship, both can be conducted in a manner that is praised when they are called scientific.

The word "science" derives from the Latin word *scientia*, for which the Greek equivalent is either *epistēmē* or *doxa*. In antiquity and the Middle Ages, the various branches of philosophy were called sciences. Today, from the point of view of the empirical sciences, when philosophers employ a praiseworthy method they are called scientific. (*See* the entry under Knowledge.)

With the rise of positivism in the nineteenth and twentieth centuries, which asserts that empirically reliable knowledge is to be found only in the empirical and experimental sciences, it has become necessary to set investigative science apart from history, from mathematics, and from philosophy.

I have explained elsewhere in what manner the branches of philosophy, especially metaphysics (or philosophical theology) and philosophical psychology, can be properly compared with the empirical and experimental sciences with regard to agreement and disagreement, progress, and the criteria of truth and falsity.

It is of great interest that all the disciplines being compared (the empirical sciences, mathematics, history, and philosophy) have a history and a philosophy, but no science (in the modern, positivistic sense) that is applicable to the understanding of the sciences themselves. *There is no science of science.*

Earlier, I wrote a methodological account of philosophy's past, present, and future. There I explained why philosophy has been so late in maturing. Philosophy has a brighter future in the centuries ahead.

If philosophy did not exist, we would have no moral philosophy as a branch of knowledge and we would have no understanding of science itself, for when scientists write about science, they do so as philosophers, not as scientists.

SENSE This word is used as an abbreviation of what more accurately should be designated our human sensitive powers.

The comprehensive enumeration of our sensitive powers, or what may also be called our powers of perceptual thought, include sensation itself, both externally and peripherally. It also includes our sensitive memory and our imagination.

Since we also have the power of conceptual thought, it may be asked whether these two sets of powers cooperate or function independently of each other. Our intellectual powers are dependent on our imagination. What in the Middle Ages was called a phantasm is a necessary but not a sufficient condition of conceptual thought. That dependence is a causal dependence.

Purely intellectual activity cannot occur without some action by our sensitive powers, but the content of conceptual thought is not affected by it. We can think conceptually of that which is not sensible at all, and not imaginable.

The dependence of our sensitive powers upon our intellects is of a different order. The content of perceptual thought is always affected by the action of our intellects simultaneously. Persons who are conceptually blind in one or another of their peripheral sense organs can exercise the conceptually blind sense organ without knowing what it is they are sensing. They can, for example, smell a rose that is put under their nose, but not know that it is a rose they are smelling.

What is sometimes called the intellectual imagination represents the simultaneous activity of both sensitive and intellectual powers. It is impossible for us to experience the world around us as brute animals experience it, with only sensitive powers and no intellects. For us it is a meaningful world; for them, it is meaningless.

SIN The word "sin" is used loosely in everyday speech, but its only appropriate meaning becomes clear when sins are distinguished from crimes. In that clear usage, a sin is an act of disobedience to God, a violation of the Ten Commandments or of Christ's two precepts of charity.

One and the same act may be a violation of both divine law and human law, but it is a sin only if it is an act of disobedience to God's commandments or precepts. It is a crime only with regard to human positive law. We cannot sin against our human neighbors even when we treat them unjustly.

In the Lord's Prayer, we ask to be forgiven for our trespasses as we forgive those who trespass against us. We cannot ask to be forgiven by God for sinning against other human beings.

You may ask about violations of the natural, as distinct from the positive, law. Such violations are immoral and unjust acts, and they may be both sins against God and crimes punishable by the state. (*See* the entry under Law.)

SOUL The word "soul" is used by almost everyone with the negative understanding that, unlike physical and material bodies, it represents something that is *not* physical and *not* material. But that understanding of soul, in itself and in relation to body, leaves many philosophical questions unanswered.

The most important issue in the understanding of soul occurred early in the history of philosophy. It is the difference between the views of Plato and Aristotle.

For Plato, the soul was a spiritual substance conjoined with a material or physical body. In addition, for Plato that union of soul and body occurs only in human beings. Plants, animals, and other living organisms do not have souls.

In the Platonic view, the immortality of the human soul is self-evident, or at least easily demonstrated, because when death occurs, the soul, being a simple substance, is released and continues in existence.

Wordsworth's "Ode on the Intimations of Immortality" speaks of the soul as coming from heaven, which is its home; and refers to the body as "the prison house of the soul."

The Platonic doctrine of body and soul takes on another form in modern times with Descartes's distinction between *res extensa* and *res cogitans*. As for Plato, so for Descartes, the human being is an almost inexplicable union of two separate substances—body and mind. Since Descartes, the mind–body problem has obsessed modern philosophy. As stated by Descartes, that problem is insoluble.

For Aristotle, the word "soul" names the form to be found in the substance of all living matter. A living organism, as opposed to an inanimate substance, is "besouled"—which is to say "alive." These two words are interchangeable.

For Aristotle, the question of the immortality of the human soul is not raised, even though Aristotle declares that the intellect, which is one of the soul's specific powers, is immortal because it is immaterial. However, when Christian theologians consider the immortality of the human soul, they must also affirm the resurrection of the body, because the imagination is a necessary but not a sufficient condition for the exercise of human conceptual thought.

From the purely philosophical as opposed to the theological point of view, the most that can be said is that the immortality of the human soul is possible, but its actuality cannot be philosophically demonstrated.

SPIRIT This word is generally used in everyday speech by persons who cannot tell you in positive terms what they mean by it. If you ask them for a synonym, they cannot give it to you. They have only some vague idea of what they are referring to.

Philosophically, the only precise meaning of the words "spirit" and "spiritual" is negative, not positive. What is spiritual is immaterial. God is spiritual, the angels are spirits, and the human intellect—the intellect, not the soul—is a spiritual power, which is to say it is immaterial. (*See* the entries under Man and under Soul.)

STATE The word "state" is used loosely in everyone's daily speech. It requires qualification for philosophy's purposes.

Used loosely, it refers to any community of individuals who live peaceably with one another for their common good—people who for the most part are not related in any way by ties of blood or of consanguinity. In this sense of the word, the fifty states that are members of the American union are states, and so too is the United States of America.

However, the fifty states of the American union are not properly called states, because they do not have any external sovereignty; they cannot make war and peace with foreign communities; they cannot make alliances with them, or enter into treaties with them.

Philosophically, a state can be said to exist only when it is a community ruled by a person or persons who hold public office or offices that are defined by a constitution that the community has formulated and ratified. Another word for such a community, in which the rulers have no power vested in them personally, but only in the offices to which they have been elected or appointed, is a "republic." In this sense of the term, a community ruled by a king or despot is not a state.

Aristotle puts his finger on this point of difference between communities that are and communities that are not states in which the rulers are either elected or appointed officeholders. The citizens are those who rule and are ruled in turn—rulers when they are public officials and ruled when they are returned to private life as citizens no longer in office.

In ancient Greece the city (or *polis*) was a state or republic. The word "citizen" derives its meaning from that fact.

Only a person who is governed constitutionally is properly called a citizen. If the constitutionally governed communities of Greek antiquity had been called "republics" instead of "city-states," the word "republican" could have been used instead of "citizen."

In the world today most of its population lives under dictatorships, not in republics. A very small percentage of the world's population lives in states that are clearly republics.

THEOLOGY The word "theology" loosely used stands, as its etymology makes clear, for any knowledge of God. For philosophical purposes, it is necessary to distinguish three kinds of theology, one of which really is not theology at all, but often parades as if it were.

In the three religions of the West (Judaism, Christianity, and Islam) there is what should be called dogmatic or sacred theology—sacred because it is based on the revealed word of God in sacred scriptures, and dogmatic because it deals with a religion's articles of faith, dogmatically declared.

Such sacred and dogmatic theology is called by Thomas Aquinas the queen of the sciences, and philosophy is her handmaiden. The thinking that is done by the philosopher in sacred theology is directed by religious faith; and the process by which sacred theology is developed can be described as faith seeking understanding. The role Thomas Aquinas played in Christian theology is played by Moses Maimonides in Jewish sacred theology, and by Avicenna in the sacred theology of Islam.

Philosophical theology, neither sacred nor dogmatic, represents thinking about God that is done by pagans—persons without religious faith, or at least by individuals who do not appeal to the articles of any religious faith. My book *How to Think About God* (1980) was written when I was still a pagan. It was written for pagans. I must confess that the thinking I did in writing that book was influential in my becoming a Christian in 1984.

The third mode of theology has often been called natural theology, but unlike philosophical theology, it is a body of purely natural knowledge with no appeals to dogmas or articles of faith. What is traditionally called natural theology is really apologetics, Christian, Jewish, or Islamic. It is a defense of the faith by persons who have that faith, and it is addressed to those who do not share that faith.

The *Summa Theologica* of Thomas Aquinas is

a work in sacred theology. He wrote another series of volumes entitled *Summa Contra Gentiles,*
addressed to the Moors and Jews in Spain, attempting to persuade them that the Christian
faith he was defending is the one true faith, and
should be adopted by them. That is a work in
Christian apologetics.

The English bishop William Paley wrote a
work in Christian apologetics, and so too did
John Locke. The titles of their books are, respectively, *A View of the Evidence of Christianity*
(1794) and *The Reasonableness of Christianity*
(1731).

The literature on this subject would be clarified if such works were acknowledged as Christian apologetics, instead of claiming to be
natural theology. The latter term should be re-
served for works in philosophical theology that
should always be pagan in their character for
both writers and readers.

TIME The word "time" names one of the four dimensions in the theory of relativity. The dimension of time together with the three special

dimensions is what is called the four-dimensional manifold. For theoretical physicists the word has changed its meaning since the time of Isaac Newton. For Newton, time and space were absolute dimensions, but for Albert Einstein, time is relative to the other three basic dimensions.

Einstein said that only time, as measurable by physicists, should interest them; but in his book *A Brief History of Time* (1988), the contemporary astrophysicist Stephen W. Hawking made a very questionable statement. He said that time not measurable by physicists does not exist in reality.

In saying this he contradicted himself by the title of his book. Hawking's book is brief, but that brief period is psychological time, a period of time that is *not* measurable by physicists.

At this point philosophers should intervene: *in the first place,* because in philosophical theology, we must assume that time is everlasting—without beginning or end—whether any portion of this time is or is not measurable by physicists; *in the second place,* because time considered philosophically is the duration in which change does occur. The opposite of everlasting time is eternity, conceived as the sphere of the immutable, the timeless.

Readers will find a most interesting discussion of our psychological experience of time, in itself and in its relation to eternity, in Book XI of St. Augustine's *Confessions*. Eternity is, of course, not experienceable by us at all.

The psychological experience of time that Augustine discusses is certainly not the same as the time measurable by contemporary physicists, but that it has reality is beyond question.

TOTALITARIANISM The word "totalitarianism" was first used in the twentieth century by Hannah Arendt in a book entitled *Origins of Totalitarianism* (1951). But the first appearance of the concept, if not the word, occurred in 1835 in Alexis de Tocqueville's *Democracy in America*.

Chapter VI of Part Four in that work is entitled "What Sort of Despotism Democratic Nations Have to Fear." There he says:

> I think, then, that the species of oppression by which democratic nations are menaced is unlike anything which ever before existed in the world;

our contemporaries will find no prototype of it in their memories. I seek in vain for an expression which will accurately convey the whole of the idea I have formed of it; the old words "despotism" and "tyranny" are inappropriate. The thing itself is new, and, since I cannot name [it], I must attempt to define it.

Tocqueville not only had the correct idea of the despotism he feared might arise in the future, but he also had an understanding of how it might come about. He pointed out that the despotism of Louis XIV in France arose when the monarch commanded all the nobles of France to live at Versailles, whereas previously they represented secondary instruments of government by ruling in their feudal domains. The despotism of the king was thus alleviated.

Tocqueville proposed that in the democracies of the future, associations of private citizens should function as secondary instruments of government, to avoid a similar concentration of power. He developed this point in Chapter VII.

Generalized, the point is expressed by Abraham Lincoln in his statement that the federal government should do for the people only those things which the people cannot do for themselves, either individually or collectively in their private associations. This is the principle of subsidiarity.

The private associations may be associations for profit or they may be philanthropic associations, but they should operate to prevent the concentration of all power, both political and economic, in the hands of the central government.

TRUTH AND TASTE The word "truth" is often used without any understanding of the difference between descriptive and prescriptive truth, and without clear differentiation between matters of truth and matters of taste.

Descriptive truth, which consists in the agreement of the mind with reality, requires affirmation of the existence of an independent reality. The modern error of ontological idealism must be corrected. (*See* the entry under Reality and Appearance.)

Prescriptive truth consists in the agreement of the mind with right desire.

In both cases it is important to distinguish between the *definition* of truth and the *criteria* employed in testing whether a given proposition or judgment is true or false, either beyond the shadow of a doubt, or beyond a reasonable doubt, or by a preponderance of reason and evidence, at the time the proposition (as entertained or judged) has certitude, or has some degree of probability.

In addition to the tests of truth that depend on the agreement of the mind with reality or right desire, there is the test of coherence. If the human mind is confronted with an incompatibility between its prior judgments and a new judgment, it must seek intrinsic coherence or compatibility by choosing between its earlier judgments and the new one. In short, the mind must choose between its earlier hypotheses and a new hypothesis that calls for consideration. The test of coherence is governed by the principle of incompatibility.

There is one further consideration, and that is the distinction between matters of truth and matters of taste. If anything is a matter of truth, it is transculturally true. The truths of mathematics, of theoretical physics, and all the other empirical natural sciences are transcultural in this sense.

But there is still a question about whether the claims of philosophy, of history, and of the social sciences can be similarly regarded. All that we can say at present is that philosophy's claim to get at the truth is to be regarded as transcultural, not just a matter of taste that will always differ from one culture to another.

To deny philosophy this claim while according it to the empirical or experimental sciences is merely another token of the positivism that prevails throughout the world at the end of the twentieth century.

No one doubts that the natural sciences have transcultural truth. Few believe that philosophy does. Philosophy will achieve the status it should have, and in my judgment can have, only when it succeeds in justifying its claim to be in the sphere of truth rather than the sphere of taste.

VIRTUE AND VICE These two words as used in everyday speech have acquired strange and even wrong meanings. The word "virtue," for example, is still often identified with a woman's chastity, though with the advent of the women's liberation movement, that strange meaning either has disappeared or will soon do so.

From a philosophical point of view, the words "virtue" and "vice" are definitely misused when they are used in the plural. Most people think that there are many virtues and vices, and that it is possible for a person to be virtuous in certain respects, though not in others.

In the first place, we must distinguish between intellectual virtues (in the plural) and moral virtue (in the singular). There are five intellectual virtues, three of them in the sphere of knowing (science, understanding, and wisdom) and two of them in the sphere of making and acting (skill and prudence). It is possible to have one or another of these intellectual virtues without having all of them. Prudence, which is sometimes called practical wisdom, is also one of the four cardinal aspects of moral virtue (temperance, courage or fortitude, justice, and prudence).

Readers should note that I referred to the aforementioned aspects of moral virtue, not to them as if they were existentially separate virtues: as if we could be temperate without also being courageous, or as if we could be just without also being prudent.

The basic point here is that moral virtue is one habit—a habit of right desire that has four distinct but existentially inseparable aspects. Moral virtue is acquired and formed by repeated morally good acts. But an individual who possesses the habit of moral virtue to any degree may commit morally wrong acts without losing his or her moral virtue. The habit may be weakened by such wrongful actions if they are committed too frequently, just as it may be strengthened and fortified by repeated morally good acts.

Aristotle's *Nicomachean Ethics* is the only sound, practical, and undogmatic moral philosophy in which the pivotal notion is habit. It is a moral philosophy without rules.

Aristotle is the only philosopher who affirms the unity of moral virtue, and thus explains how moral virtue is at once self-regarding and other-regarding, at once selfish in its motivation and altruistic.

For our own good, our own happiness, we have to be temperate and courageous, and for the happiness of others, we have to be just in our habitual actions toward them. The other basic notions in Aristotle's ethics are real and apparent goods, needs, and wants (natural and acquired desires).

WAR AND PEACE   The word "war" in everyday discourse usually means actual warfare, fighting with whatever weapons are available at the time and place, and the word "peace" usually means the opposite, the absence of violent warfare.

But, considered philosophically, we must take account of a more complex set of meanings. In the first place we must distinguish between the state of war and actual warfare. Sovereign princes or sovereign states in relation to one another are in a condition of anarchy. In this century we have a new name for this condition. We have called it the "cold war," as opposed to the hot condition of actual warfare. In the "cold war" with each other, sovereign states may be *either* friendly *or* hostile, but that relationship can change from time to time.

The word "peace," in addition to its negative meaning as an absence of the violence of actual warfare, has a positive meaning. Civil peace is enjoyed by a people who can settle all their conflicts and disputes by means of the instrumentalities of government and law, and so they do not have to resort to the violence of actual warfare.

We owe to the philosopher Thomas Hobbes

this more precise understanding of war and peace. It is this more precise understanding that leads us to the conclusion that, in the absence of government, which is anarchy, we cannot have civil peace, locally, nationally, or in the world of international relations. Permanent world peace without world civil government is impossible.

WILL This word names a human faculty, appetitive in character. As our intellect is a cognitive power, so our will is an appetitive power. For those who think of will power as a faculty that is sensitive in character, and is possessed by the higher mammals as well as by human beings, it is necessary to correct their view of will by saying, philosophically, that will is an intellectual appetite and, as such, is immaterial just as the intellect is immaterial.

The freedom of the will is a freedom of choice. It consists in our being able to choose otherwise, no matter how we do choose.

197

WORLD In everyday speech this word is often used as a synonym for this planet in the solar system. Philosophically, it is used as a synonym for the cosmos or physical universe. The best philosophical use of the word "world" is to designate all of reality, both physical and sensible and also intelligible and immaterial. In philosophical theology as well as in sacred or dogmatic theology, the world consists of the totality of God's creatures, but does not include God. Even if the world or cosmos had never been created, God would have real existence.

WORLD GOVERNMENT *See* the entry under War and Peace.

Appendices

Appendix I

NOTES FOR CONTINUED DISCUSSION

BEATITUDE
> *A Vision of the Future* (1984), Chapter 2, especially pages 29–30.

BEAUTY
> *Six Great Ideas* (1981, 1984), Chapters 5, 16, and 17.

BEING
> *The Four Dimensions of Philosophy* (1993, 1994), especially Chapter 8, pages 89–105.

BELIEF
> *Truth in Religion* (1990, 1992), Chapter 9.

CAPITALISM AND SOCIALISM
> *Haves Without Have-Nots* (1991), Part One, entitled "The End of the Conflict Between Capitalism and Communism."

CASUISTRY
> *Desires, Right & Wrong* (1991), Chapter 5, entitled "Fundamental Errors in Moral Philosophy"; Appendix I, Notes 9 and 10, pages 148–157.

CERTAINTY AND PROBABILITY
> *Ten Philosophical Mistakes* (1985, 1987), Chapter 7, entitled "Freedom of Choice."

CITIZEN
> *A Vision of the Future* (1984), Chapters 6 and 7.

COGNITION
> *Some Questions About Language* (1976, 1991), Chapter IV, Question 6.

COMMON GOOD
> *The Common Sense of Politics* (1971, 1996), Chapters 10–12.

CONSTITUTION
A Vision of the Future (1984), Chapter 6; *Haves Without Have-Nots* (1991), Part Four, entitled "Lincoln's Declaration."

CONTEMPLATION
Desires, Right & Wrong (1991), Chapter 5, pages 78–95.

CONTINENCE AND INCONTINENCE
Desires, Right & Wrong (1991), Chapter 3 and Chapter 6, especially page 100.

DEMOCRACY
The Common Sense of Politics (1971, 1996), Chapters 9–13.

DOGMATISM
Truth in Religion (1990, 1992).

EDUCATION
(On Behalf of the Paideia Group) *The Paideia Proposal* (1982); (with Members of the Paideia Group) *The Paideia Program* (1984); *Reforming Education* (1988, 1990), Chapters 12–15, and Chapters 21–24; and *A Second Look in the Rearview Mirror* (1992, 1994), Chapter 4.

EQUALITY AND INEQUALITY
Six Great Ideas (1981, 1984), Chapters 21–23.

GOD
How to Think About God (1980, 1982, 1988, 1991), especially Chapter 9.

GOOD AND EVIL
Six Great Ideas (1981, 1984), especially Chapters 10–12.

GOVERNMENT
A Vision of the Future (1984), especially Chapters 6 and 7.

HAPPINESS
A Vision of the Future (1984), Chapter 4.

HIERARCHY
Problems of Thomists: The Problem of Species (1940); "Solution of the Problem of Species" (1941).

HUMAN NATURE AND NURTURE
Ten Philosophical Mistakes (1985, 1987), Chapter 8.

INFINITY
How to Think About God (1980, 1982, 1988, 1991), Chapter 9, pages 87–88.

LABOR
A Vision of the Future (1984), Chapter 2.

LANGUAGE
Some Questions About Language (1976, 1991), Chapter III.

LEISURE
A Vision of the Future (1984), Chapter 2.

LIBERAL ARTS
(On Behalf of the Paideia Group) *The Paideia Proposal* (1982) and (with Members of the Paideia Group) *The Paideia Program* (1984).

LIBERTY
Six Great Ideas (1981, 1984), Chapters 19 and 20.

MACHINE
Intellect: Mind Over Matter (1990, 1993), Chapters 4 and 5; *The Difference of Man and the Difference It Makes* (1967, 1993), Chapters 2, 13–14.

MAN
   The Difference of Man and the Difference It Makes (1967, 1993), Chapter 2.
MEDICINE
   Reforming Education (1988, 1990), Chapter 12, especially pages 169–172.
MEMORY AND IMAGINATION
   Some Questions About Language (1976, 1991), Chapter VII.
METAPHYSICS
   The Four Dimensions of Philosophy (1993, 1994), page 76.
NOMINALISM
   Ten Philosophical Mistakes (1985, 1987), Chapter 2, especially pages 37–45.
OBJECTIVE AND SUBJECTIVE
   Six Great Ideas (1981, 1984), Chapter 6.
OPINION
   Six Great Ideas (1981, 1984), Chapter 7.
PHILOSOPHY
   The Four Dimensions of Philosophy (1993, 1994), Chapters 8–13.
PLEASURE AND PAIN
   Desires, Right & Wrong (1991), Chapter 3, pages 38–45, and Appendix I, Note 1, pages 125–126.
POETRY
   A Guidebook to Learning (1986), Chapter 14, pages 124–127 (relation of poetry to history and philosophy).
PRIVATE PROPERTY
   Haves Without Have-Nots (1991), Part One, entitled

"The End of the Conflict Between Capitalism and Communism," pages 9–14.

PUNISHMENT

(with Jerome Michael) *Crime, Law and Social Science* (1933, 1971), Chapter XII, Sections 1–4.

REALITY AND APPEARANCE

The Four Dimensions of Philosophy (1993, 1994), Chapters 8–9, and *Intellect: Mind Over Matter* (1990, 1993) (discussion of treatment of appearances by critical realists).

RIGHTS, NATURAL AND CIVIL

Desires, Right & Wrong (1991), Epilogue, entitled "Transcultural Ethics"; *The Time of Our Lives* (1970, 1996), Chapter 14.

SCIENCE

The Four Dimensions of Philosophy (1993, 1994) and *Ten Philosophical Mistakes* (1985, 1987), Epilogue, entitled "Modern Science and Ancient Wisdom."

SENSE

Intellect: Mind Over Matter (1990, 1993), Chapter 3, pages 35–40.

SOUL

Aristotle for Everybody (1978, 1980, 1991), Chapter 22, and *Intellect: Mind Over Matter* (1990, 1993), Chapter 4.

STATE

The Common Sense of Politics (1971, 1996), Chapters 7 and 8.

THEOLOGY
>   *A Second Look in the Rearview Mirror* (1992, 1994),
>   Chapter 9, entitled "A Philosopher's Religious Faith."

TIME
>   *How to Think About God* (1980, 1982, 1988, 1991),
>   Chapter 4.

TOTALITARIANISM
>   *A Vision of the Future* (1984), Chapter 5, pages
>   132–136; Chapter 6, pages 174–178; Chapter 7, pages
>   210–217, 222–253.

TRUTH AND TASTE
>   *Six Great Ideas* (1981, 1984), Chapters 5–7, 10, 11, and
>   26; *Ten Philosophical Mistakes* (1985, 1987), Chapter
>   5; *The Four Dimensions of Philosophy* (1993, 1994),
>   especially Chapters 5, 7, and Epilogue; and *Truth in
>   Religion* (1990, 1992), Chapter 1 and Appendix, enti-
>   tled "The Unity of Man and the Unity of Truth,"
>   pages 113–114.

VIRTUE AND VICE
>   *Desires, Right & Wrong* (1991).

WAR AND PEACE
>   *How to Think About War and Peace* (1944, 1995); *The
>   Common Sense of Politics* (1971, 1996), Chapter 16.

WILL
>   *Ten Philosophical Mistakes* (1985, 1987), Chapter 7
>   (ampler discussion of freedom of choice).

WORLD GOVERNMENT
>   *Haves Without Have-Nots* (1991), Part Six, entitled
>   "The New World of the Twenty-first Century: USDR."

Appendix II

CITED WORKS BY MORTIMER ADLER

The Angels and Us, New York: Macmillan, 1982; Collier Books, 1988, 1993.

Aristotle for Everybody: Difficult Thought Made Easy, New York: Macmillan, 1978; Bantam Books, 1980; Collier Books, 1991.

Art, the Arts, and the Great Ideas, New York: Macmillan, 1994; Touchstone, 1995.

The Common Sense of Politics (based on the Encyclopædia Britannica Lectures delivered at the University of Chicago, 1970), New York: Holt, Rinehart and Winston, 1971; to be republished with a new Introduction by John Van Doren (Bronx, N.Y.: Fordham University Press, 1996).

The Conditions of Philosophy: Its Checkered Past, Its Present Disorder, and Its Future Promise (based on the Encyclopædia Britannica Lectures delivered at the University of Chicago, 1964). New York: Atheneum Publishers, 1965; New York: Delta Books, Dell Publishing, 1967.

(with Jerome Michael) *Crime, Law and Social Science*, London: Kegan Paul, Trench, Trubner, and New York: Harcourt, Brace, 1933; reprinted with Introduction by Gilbert Geis, Montclair, N.J.: Patterson Smith, 1971.

Desires, Right & Wrong: The Ethics of Enough, New York: Macmillan, 1991.

The Difference of Man and the Difference It Makes (based on the Encyclopædia Britannica Lectures delivered at the University of Chicago, 1966), Introduction by Theodore T. Puck, New York: Holt, Rinehart and Winston, 1967; republished with new Introduction by Deal W. Hudson, Bronx, N.Y.: Fordham University Press, 1993.

The Four Dimensions of Philosophy, New York: Macmillan, 1993; Collier Books, 1994.

A Guidebook to Learning: For a Lifelong Pursuit of Wisdom, New York: Macmillan, 1986.

Haves Without Have-Nots: Essays for the 21st Century on Democracy and Socialism, New York: Macmillan, 1991.

How to Think About God: A Guide for the 20th-Century Pagan, New York: Macmillan, 1980; Bantam Books, 1982, 1988; Collier Books, 1991.

How to Think About War and Peace, New York: Simon and Schuster, 1944; to be republished with a new Introduction by John J. Logue (Bronx, N.Y.: Fordham University Press, 1995).

The Idea of Freedom: A Dialectical Examination of the Conceptions of Freedom, Volume I, Garden City, N.Y.: Doubleday, 1958; reprinted Westport, Conn.: Greenwood Press, 1973.

The Idea of Freedom: A Dialectical Examination of the Controversies About Freedom, Volume II, Garden City, N.Y.: Doubleday, 1961; reprinted Westport, Conn.: Greenwood Press, 1973.

Intellect: Mind Over Matter, New York: Macmillan, 1990; Collier Books, 1993.

(On Behalf of the Paideia Group) *The Paideia Proposal: An Educational Manifesto,* New York: Collier Books, Macmillan, 1982.

(with Members of the Paideia Group) *The Paideia Program: An Educational Syllabus,* New York: Collier Books, Macmillan, 1984.

Problems for Thomists: The Problem of Species, New York: Sheed & Ward, 1940.

Reforming Education: The Opening of the American Mind, edited by Geraldine Van Doren, New York: Macmillan, 1988; Collier Books, 1990.

A Second Look in the Rearview Mirror, New York: Macmillan, 1992; Collier Books, 1994.

Six Great Ideas, New York: Macmillan, 1981; Collier Books, 1984.

"Solution of the Problem of Species," *The Thomist,* III (April 1941), 279–379.

Some Questions About Language: A Theory of Human

Discourse and Its Objects, La Salle, Ill.: Open Court, 1976; First Paperback Edition, 1991.

Ten Philosophical Mistakes, New York: Macmillan, 1985; Collier Books, 1987.

The Time of Our Lives: The Ethics of Common Sense (based on the Encyclopædia Britannica Lectures delivered at the University of Chicago, 1969), New York: Holt, Rinehart and Winston, 1970; to be republished with a new Introduction by Deal W. Hudson (Bronx, N.Y.: Fordham University Press, 1996).

Truth in Religion: The Plurality of Religions and the Unity of Truth, New York: Macmillan, 1990; Collier Books, 1992.

A Vision of the Future: Twelve Ideas for a Better Life and a Better Society, New York: Macmillan, 1984.

Index

Page references in **boldface** refer to dictionary entries.

ontology, 80, 101–2, 151, 168, 191
opinion, **154–55**
Origins of Totalitarianism (Arendt), 189

Paideia reform, 135–36
pain, **158–59**
Paley, William, 187
parapsychology, 29
Pascal, Blaise, 28, 54
peace, **196–97**
perception, 42–43, 148
perceptual thought, 144, 151–52, 168, 178–79
Pericles, 77–78
Philosophical Dictionary, A (Voltaire), 10
philosophy, 15, **156–57**
    four dimensions of, 157
    religion vs., 170–71
    science and, 177
physical sciences, 13–14, 40, 42, 46, 145
Plato, 28, 30, 73, 116, 135, 181
pleasure, **158–59**
Poetics (Aristotle), 160
poetry, **159–61**
Politics (Aristotle), 35, 70
positivism, 150, 157, 174, 176, 193
possible, 45–46

Prince, The (Machiavelli), 113
private property, **161–63**
probability, 53–57
progress, **164–66**
prose, 159–60
Ptolemy, 105
punishment, **166–68**

Quakers, 61–62
quantum electrodynamics (QED), 145

realism, 41, 168
reality, 39–43, **168–69**
reason, 75, 88
relative, **13–15**
relativity, 187–88
religion, **169–71**
    angels and, **27–31**
    belief and, **46–48**
    civil disobedience based on, 61–62
    contemplation and, 74
    heaven and hell in, **105–7**
    immortality and, **119–120**
    law and, 131, 132
    philosophy vs., 170–71
    see also God; theology; *specific religions*
remorse, 75